PRACTICAL SOCIAL WORK
Series Editor: Jo Campling

[BASW]

Editorial Advisory Board:
Terry Bamford, Malcolm Payne, Patrick Phelan,
Peter Riches, Jane Tunstill
and Sue Walrond-Skinner

Social work is at an important stage in its development. All professions must be responsive to changing social and economic conditions if they are to meet the needs of those they serve. This series focuses on sound practice and the specific contribution which social workers can make to the well-being of our society in the 1980s.

The British Association of Social Workers has always been conscious of its role in setting guidelines for practice and in seeking to raise professional standards. The conception of the Practical Social Work series arose from a survey of BASW members to discover where they, the practitioners in social work, felt there was the most need for new literature. The response was overwhelming and enthusiastic, and the result is a carefully planned, coherent series of books. The emphasis is firmly on practice, set in a theoretical framework. The books will inform, stimulate and promote discussion, thus adding to the further development of skills and high professional standards. All the authors are practitioners and teachers of social work representing a wide variety of experience.

JO CAMPLING

PRACTICAL SOCIAL WORK

Series Editor: Jo Campling

BASW

Student Supervision

Kathy Ford and Alan Jones

**MACMILLAN
EDUCATION**

First published 1987

Published by
MACMILLAN EDUCATION LTD
Houndmills, Basingstoke, Hampshire RG21 2XS
and London
Companies and representatives
throughout the world

Printed in Hong Kong

British Library Cataloguing in Publication Data
Ford, Kathy
Student supervision.—(BASW practical
social work)
1. Supervision of social workers
2. Occupational training—Great Britain
3. Social workers—Great Britain
I. Title   II. Jones, Alan   III. Series
361'.007'1141   HV245
ISBN 0–333–37672–2 (hardcover)
ISBN 0–333–37673–0 (paperback)

To Bruce, my friend and colleagues,
past and present.
And to Marsha, Emma and Matthew

Contents

Preface

This book arises from our shared experience over the past six years of teaching preparation courses to prospective supervisors. It is intended as a guide to the practice of supervising social work students in placement, and for this reason we present practice teaching from the supervisor's perspective. Our aim is to explain as clearly as possible the role of a supervisor as we understand it, and to suggest practical ways in which it can be carried out creatively, through such methods as role play. We hope it will prove useful to prospective supervisors, those established in the role and those who are responsible for organising preparation courses. We bring to our writing the roles of tutor, practice teacher and student. We are both qualified social workers and as ex-students have experienced the student role ourselves. We are very grateful to the members of our various supervisors' courses for contributing to our learning and for allowing us to .se the results of their learning.

Two major themes have influenced our approach to this book: first, that any practice placement should be seen in the context of a learning continuum for the individual student; second, that supervision should be seen as an active, participative partnership between the student and the supervisor, offering both the stimulation of new learning. We hope that these themes are reflected in the content. Understandably, because of the nature of our own post-qualifying experiences, the content of the book tends to reflect supervision in fieldwork in social services departments, but we believe that the ideas are equally relevant to supervision in other settings, such as group care and community work.

We have used the terms 'practice teacher' and 'supervisor' interchangeably, partly because they are in common usage and partly for variety. We understand the role implications of the different titles and that they emphasise the somewhat different, but complementary, tasks involved in them. We have also attempted to write in a non-sexist style of language throughout the book. We believe that to attempt to do this is important and also consistent with some of the ideas we promote in the book.

Although throughout this book we emphasise the desirable, necessary conditions of the agency and the attributes of the practice teacher for a successful placement, we do not wish to appear naive about the deficits in the existing system. Surveys of placements frequently indicate overcrowded conditions in agencies, poor facilities for students, lack of adequate resources and of hard pressed supervisors who lack a reduction in their own workloads in order to take students on placement. These are matters which must be tackled if students are to gain satisfactory placements in agencies. Unfortunately, these are often the same conditions shared by the full-time staff themselves. We do not pretend to have answers to these problems; indeed perhaps it is a reasonable limitation of a book with this particular focus to fail to provide them. Solutions are beyond the well-intentioned efforts of individual supervisors or tutors and will require the collaborative efforts of the Central Council for Education and Training in Social Work (CCETSW), the social work agencies and courses. Initiatives are already beginning to take place, and perhaps the proposed longer, new form of training will give fresh impetus to place practice placements on a sounder footing. Nevertheless, not all agencies have these difficulties, and even where they do exist it is clear that many satisfactory placements are still provided for social work students, and that supervisors strive to improve the quality of the experience offered to them. It is heartening that so many colleagues of supervisors are also welcoming and supportive of students placed in their teams. A more than usual amount of reference is made in the book to the influence of the University of Leicester School of Social Work. This is understandable, since both authors have been closely associated with practice developments within it and the supervisors' courses were conducted for it. Our thanks go to colleagues who, through discussion and allowing us access to their unpublished work, have contributed to the development of our thinking.

We would like to give particular thanks to Martin Shaw for reading the early draft in its entirety and giving us helpful encouragement and advice. We, of course, take full responsibility for the final result. We would also like to thank and acknowledge our profound debt to Sheila Wesson for typing the various drafts so efficiently.

KATHY FORD
ALAN JONES

1

The Transition from Practitioner to Practice Teacher

The main aim of an agency placement is to provide the aspiring entrant to social work with a protected and guided experience of contemporary social work practice in a particular service setting. The individuals who provide the protection, guidance and control we term 'supervisors' or 'practice teachers'. They are invariably social workers themselves, who are allowed to undertake the responsibility because they are qualified by training, expertise, preparation and endorsement by agency management.

In deciding to become a student supervisor a social worker is making a role transition from practitioner to teacher. Our aim is to help the aspiring supervisor, and the social worker who is already established in the role, to understand the implications of the change in role and to achieve competence in it. While poor practitioners will not make good supervisors, it does not follow that competent practitioners will automatically make skilful practice teachers, because further knowledge and skills are required for the latter role. The objectives of this chapter are:

1. To draw attention to the implications for the supervisor in undertaking this role.
2. To explore the educational, professional and organisational contexts in which this role is undertaken.
3. To introduce some useful ideas about the new role, which hopefully will stimulate curiosity and encourage a desire to become competent in it.

Practice teachers can regard themselves as having come full cycle in their careers. They have developed from perhaps unqualified practitioners, to social workers in training (the role traditionally referred to as student) and subsequently qualified practitioners, then to the role of teachers to a new generation of aspiring entrants to the profession or, as some would prefer, the occupation of social work (Toren, 1972). They have decided to play an important part in the education and training of social workers. To take on this new role successfully, it is necessary for practice teachers to enlarge their range of existing professional skills to include those of the teacher. Practitioners who want to become supervisors need to acquire knowledge about teaching and learning skills, to discover how other people learn, and how they themselves can prepare to be effective guides and teachers.

Throughout the book we use the terms 'supervisor' and 'practice teacher' as interchangeable designations of the role. We do this partly to acknowledge the fact that the terms are used commonly and interchangeably in social work education and training and also to introduce some variety in usage in the book. The terms also highlight a number of important aspects of the role, which complement each other in the work. The terms 'supervisor' and 'practice teacher' most importantly indicate the different but complementary responsibilities to the agency and to the social work course respectively. The 'supervisor' is responsible to the agency for ensuring accountability for the work, the protection of clients' interests, and the maintenance of an adequate standard of service to the clients served through the student. The 'practice teacher' is responsible to the social work course for ensuring that the student has opportunities for practice and learning, and that both are performed to a sufficient standard for the student to continue in his or her training.

The prospective practice teacher

Prospective practice teachers have listed the following desirable features in a practice teacher, on the basis of their experience as students (School of Social Work, 1983):

(a) A similar orientation to practice as the student.
(b) A personality that does not clash with theirs.
(c) They should be adequate practitioners.
(d) Knowledge of the teaching content of the course.
(e) An ability to communicate clearly.
(f) An ability to boost confidence and to give praise for competence.
(g) To be sensitive in giving criticism.
(h) To be able to create a positive working climate, recognising that a student needs to be valued by the team, by the supervisor and by the agency.
(i) To be open to a different point of view coming from the student.
(j) To have insight into a student's special needs arising out of their role and situation as a new learner.
(k) A willingness to avoid over-protectiveness.
(l) Avoidance of games playing.
(m) Avoiding 'caseworking' the student.
(n) The ability to maximise the student's learning.
(o) A need for honesty and self-awareness in a supervisor in order to enable mutual trust to develop.
(p) A willingness to be an active participant.
(q) The capacity to enjoy supervising.
(r) A willingness to make the appraisal of the student an open one, providing a different point of view with evidence to support it.
(s) An understanding of the two aspects of their role, both as practice teacher and as a supervisor of the work of the agency.

Such a list suggests that taking on the responsibility of providing a learning opportunity for another person requires thought about whether student and supervisor need to have similar outlooks, competence, and the reciprocal nature of the relationship. Also, the necessity to be a facilitating and enabling person, an awareness of the responsibilities of supervising, and a clear idea of the expectations that are to be placed on the student.

Educational issues

The great majority of social work services are provided within the state sector, with voluntary agencies playing a small but significant role. It is the responsibility of contemporary social work education and training to prepare a new generation of social workers to learn to do their jobs in a way which is both practically effective and ethically principled.

If, as Towle (1954) suggests, it is characteristic of a profession that it teaches a body of principles rather than rule-of-thumb procedures or simple routine skills, then it says something about the requirements of the people who are required to transmit that practice culture.

Overall, as Prins (undated) has suggested, social work has need of people who can combine well-educated, principled and humanitarian outlooks with technical and disciplined competence in method.

The educationist A. N. Whitehead (1950) has suggested that the process of education involves developing the following capacities in the student:

1. Evoking curiosity and judgement. If the student is properly motivated, the work should serve that function on behalf of the practice teacher.
2. The power of mastering a complicated set of circumstances. This corresponds very much to the social work task.
3. The use of theory in giving guidance in special cases. In many interventions in social work practice it would be sufficient for the student to use a general range of principles, methods and skills in helping clients. However, there are some complex problems and complicated interventions, e.g. child abuse, some behavioural programmes, family therapies, etc., in which students require additional teaching in theory and method if they are to be successful.

Practice teaching is concerned, by and large, with the ordinary, normal challenges and problems of adult learning. Adult learners have different expectations of themselves and other people than, say, children (Knowles, 1973). They are sometimes people of considerable life experience who are able to bring this to bear on their work and learning. They expect to be treated as the responsible and mature people they usually are. The motivation of adult learners in a professional context is influenced by the usefulness of the knowledge. Adults tend to retain for longer the knowledge which they use in their daily lives, and they are more motivated to learn things that will be useful to them (Knowles, 1973).

Learning theories in social work education

The nature of learning in social work, and thus the focus of supervision, is directed towards three aspects:

1. *The cognitive*: i.e. the ability to remember, to analyse, to reason and conceptualise in relation to problems and solutions.
2. *The affective*: i.e. the ability to feel, to value and to empathise with the emotions of other people or indeed of oneself.
3. *The behavioural*: i.e. the ability to act or carry out in a purposeful way the conclusions which derive from analysing and experiencing.

Whatever the activity in which the student is engaged, it should be possible to analyse performance as lying within one or more of these three frameworks of understanding. Similarly, if students have learning difficulties or even problems of a more serious nature, they will present themselves as failing in performance in one or more of these three areas (Towle, 1954).

While students vary in their personalities, styles of learning and approaches to work, it is suggested that there are certain recognisable phases or steps which learning follows in relation to any particular problem. These sequential steps we call the process of learning.

This process provides a useful framework for practice teachers to view the different learning situations with which their students will be faced. Furthermore, the educationist Tyler (1971) has identified what can be called the 'becoming requirements' for members of professions generally. These are broad categories of performance or behaviour which seem to be typical attributes required of professional people.

They can provide supervisors with a useful framework of outcomes within which to understand their role as teacher and from which to view the overall learning of their student. Tyler has described these requirements as follows:

1. To develop understanding of important facts and principles.
2. To develop familiarity with dependable sources of information.
3. The ability to interpret data.
4. To develop the ability to apply values that are taught to problems that arise in the work.
5. The ability to study and report the results of study.
6. The ability to apply the learning behaviours in an active and dependable way.

Teacher/learner roles

Historically, the nature and quality of the teacher/learner relationship has changed its emphasis over time; Wijnberg and Schwartz (1977) have usefully identified those changes under three categories. They identify the apprentice, growth and role-systems models, which together, it is suggested, are appropriate for contemporary social work. Davis (1984), in his recent research study of student satisfaction with their social work training, indicated that the use of the apprentice model was still prevalent. It is useful to see the three models as not only identifying the changing nature of social work and social work education over time, but also as reflecting the changing emphasis in contemporary supervision rather than requiring the supervisor to make a choice between them. The *apprentice model* emphasises what supervisors have to offer from their own knowledge, skills and experience and in particular the demands of the setting. The *growth model* developed under the influence of psychodynamic psychology in work with clients and the belief that successful therapeutic work required commensurate psychological growth in the worker:

> To believe in the possibility of growth for the client, one has to have known the rules of growth in the self, through help

consciously sought and professionally contributed (Wijnberg and Schwartz, 1977, p. 108).

The value of this perspective for contemporary practice is the notion that the supervisory relationship is one that must be congruent with the content of the work which the student has to carry out with the client.

The *role-systems model* emphasises the institutional nature of the relationship between the supervisor and student, identifying the role expectations which form their membership of the agency and the course respectively:

> In order for the role systems model to be most effective, the student's relationship to the supervisor should be based less on psychological coercion and more on the shared recognition of the supervisor's expert power 1977 (Wijnberg and Schwartz, p. 109).

However, not all expertise lies with the supervisor, and greater recognition and responsibility is placed on the student for contributing to the learning. Indeed, students enjoy the right to try out their own chosen methods of helping, arising from learning independent of the placement, as long as it is judged by the supervisor to be competent knowledge in principle, and to be appropriate to the particular circumstances of the work at hand.

The process of supervision

We have been trying to identify the knowledge which practice teachers might usefully bear in mind in considering their new role. However, in addition to those considerations, they will need to become knowledgeable and skilful about the management of the learning situation with the student. This is called the process of supervision. The management of the teaching/ learning relationship within the placement will be dealt with in more detail later, but the first responsibility of potential supervisors is to ask themselves whether they are ready to supervise. They must be willing to embrace the new role, including its separateness and difference from that of the supervisee. They need to be sufficiently secure in their own knowledge and social work practice so that they are not threatened unnecessarily by a student, and to feel they have sufficient to offer. They require an ability to conceptualise the role tasks sufficiently well to be able to convey them to the student. Supervisors also need some facility to understand the theory which supports interventive methods, so that experience and knowledge can be brought together in an understandable way for the student. In this way principles can be identified, stored in the student's accumulating understanding, and tested for their transferability in other comparable situations. Lastly, supervisors need to be open, accepting and supportive, able to create an environment in which a teaching-learning relationship can be formed and developed. The supervisory role can be seen as a final stage in the development of the professional role – that of learning to teach the art that one has acquired oneself.

Professional issues

It is in the nature of professions that they are required to provide the training for the next generation of practitioners, as they have no alternative to using their own members to do it (Johnson, 1972). Professional work requires extensive knowledge, skills and techniques and the use of discretion in implementing them appropriately. The skills in applying the knowledge and techniques appropriately have to be learned finally by applying them in the situation in which the work is eventually practised.

It has become conventional practice in social work to separate the educational and training functions which make up the package of preparation (Younghusband, 1978). The knowledge and skills required have become so extensive and diverse that there is a need for specialisation of functions. Social work agencies do not see it as their role to provide extensive preparatory education for their practitioners. It is the task of specialised education and training courses to find an appropriate balance between the systematic teaching of knowledge and the acquisition of skills through rehearsal in training.

Agency settings

The agency is the institutional context of social work. Perhaps even more than the functions of social work, the types of problems with which it deals, the populations which it serves, or the content of the knowledge base, agency settings act as the most decisive shaping force on the character and identity of social work practice (Howe, 1979).

In Britain the traditional settings or fields of practice are those of social services, probation, hospitals, voluntary agencies, etc., and they continue decisively to shape the training of social work students. These traditional agencies change in relation to the identification of new problems and needs, and also new conceptions of effective social work practice (Seebohm Report, 1968; Barclay, 1982). Indeed, new, usually smaller agencies are sometimes created and developed for the same reasons, e.g. ethnic-directed agencies serving minority ethnic communities.

Thus social work students undertake placements to learn not only the knowledge and skills of social work practice, but also how to meet the needs of clients served from a particular agency setting, and how to do so efficiently and effectively within the way the agency is organised.

Generic and generalist

It has been a widespread practice of social work courses in recent years to prepare their student social workers with what is referred to as a generic education and training. The first successful attempt to formulate an integrated model for practice was made by Bartlett (1970) in respect of casework. There have been later, influential attempts to formulate a unified or unitary model approach which can encompass all settings and methods of social work within a common framework of ideas (Goldstein, 1973; Pincus and Minahan, 1973; Middleman and Goldberg, 1974). The approaches within this broader framework attempt to apply a systems model of thinking to all the levels of intervention in social work – micro (interpersonal), mezzo (groups and communities) and macro (institutional structure). The aim is a unified approach to understanding the factors which cause and maintain social problems. In more recent thinking within the systems framework, Germain (1979, 1980) has elaborated this approach within what is termed the ecological-systems approach, with an emphasis on facilitating the mutual adaptation of individuals and their environments. Within this systems-influenced, unitary approach to practice, the knowledge and skills of each level of intervention remain relatively separate, and the implication of the approach for intervention is for a team approach to social problems in the environments in which they arise. More recently, however, a further stage in this direction of thinking has been advocated.

This argues for the development of generic skills for social work, which can be applied flexibly to each of the different levels of intervention required for a comprehensive approach to social problems. This remains undeveloped at the present time, but indicates the direction of efforts towards a comprehensive generic social work role and practice. These developments in conceptualisation and theory development in social work have had their influence on social work education and training. New entrants to social work learn both about the history of these developments and are introduced to contemporary thinking and practice through learning experiences on the course itself and in their placement settings.

The contemporary issues of sexism and racism

All personal service occupations evolve and change in response both to new responsibilities which they seek or are asked to meet and also new understandings of social problems. One example in recent times has been the 'rediscovery' and re-acceptance of poverty as a central concern for social work in Britain (Coates and Silburn, 1973).

More recently, social work, along with many other occupations, has been confronted with the issues of sexism and racism in British society generally, and in work settings in particular. If social work is to make an appropriate and successful response to the demands of these two issues, then there is a particular responsibility on the educators and trainers of new generations of social workers to take up anti-sexist and anti-racist stances in relation to their own personal work and also to ensure that this is carried through in respect of the preparation of social work students. To be fair to students, much of the intitiative, particularly in respect of sexism, has come from students themselves, particularly women students. The focus of this section is to bring to the attention of practice teachers the importance of these issues and to explore ways in which they can be furthered in the course of the placement.

Anti-sexism

Anti-sexism within social work is not simply concerned with recognising and understanding the impact of the changing role of women in British society, but also understanding, accepting and confronting:
1. The general oppression of women in a male-dominated society, where men are able to assert and maintain their dominant position through their unequal access to economic, social and political power.
2. The structured inequality experienced by women throughout all social, economic and political institutions.
3. In particular, the inequality and disadvantage they experience in relation to men in their opportunities for employment and advancement within occupations, and work within the home (Hartnett, Boden and Fuller, 1979; Mitchell and Oakley, 1976).

What are the implications for the practice teacher? Briefly, we would argue for the following changes:
1. The willingness to re-appraise conventional assumptions about gender-related issues, e.g. women's employment, the value of nursery care, expectations of women's roles, violence in the family, etc. At the very least, practice teachers should allow and, if possible, help students to explore these issues within their practice and indeed should be prepared to learn from students on these issues.
2. The recognition that women clients may want to work with women only on gender-related issues; practice teachers should be understanding of the argument that, all things

being equal, it is preferable only for women to work with women clients on gender-related issues – and, similarly, for men students to work with men clients on gender-related issues.

3. Courses should accept that women students may prefer to be supervised by women practice teachers; this should not create antagonism or defensiveness on the part of tutors or practice teachers.

4. In addition to anti-sexist practices generally in agencies, supervisors should support students' attempts to use non-sexist language in social work, whether verbally in discussions, or in writing through case records, reports to courts, etc. (Leicester University School of Social Work, 1984; Miller and Swift, 1981).

Anti-racism

For a very long time now the social, economic and political context of social work in Britain has been that of a multiracial society. There is a responsibility on the part of social workers, social work agencies and social work education to make this a reality in the work of the profession (Cheetham, 1981 and 1982). An anti-racist stance in social work generally would lead to:

1. A full acceptance of the existence of racist attitudes and practices in British society, particularly the way they disadvantage and discriminate against minority ethnic groups through the ordinary, everyday practices of its institutions.

2. A willingness to confront those institutional practices and attempt to change them towards greater social justice; and, in order to compensate for the years of injustice and reinforcement of attitudes, to pursue policies of positive discrimination and positive action.

3. The development of a racially sensitive personal social work practice, which takes fully into account the social realities faced by minority racial clients, and understands and respects different cultural beliefs, values, life-styles and goals.

These are issues which social work education and training

have to confront through a re-examination of the policies and practices of social work courses (Dominelli, 1979). They exhibit the same qualities as the many institutions they rightly teach their students to criticise. Proportionately very few black students get on to social work courses, and when they do they find that the curriculum is dominated by white, ethnocentric assumptions (CCETSW, 1983). There are few black practice teachers to service the training part of courses, and some black students suffer from cultural bias or racist assumptions in their assessments. There is little practical recognition of the wish on the part of some black students to further the welfare of their own communities when they leave the course, and they may well have supervisors who are ethnocentric in their own assumptions about good social work practice (Gullerad, 1977).

What are the implications of anti-racism for practice teachers? In our view practice teachers should:

1. State a clear preference to work only for a course which attempts an anti-racist stance.
2. Where their own knowledge is lacking, attempt to gain further training for themselves on their possibly racist beliefs and assumptions.
3. Learn more about the cultures and issues of concern to minority ethnic and racial groups with which their students may be practising.
4. Ensure that any student placed with them is required to work with minority-ethnic clients.
5. Confront the racism of white students or colleagues if this is present (Rooney, 1982).

In addition, if practice teachers should take a black student on placement with them, they should recognise the special responsibilities involved by:

1. Establishing the student's expectations of preferred practice, from simply wanting to be like any other social worker, to a desire to work predominantly with black clients.
2. Ensuring that they do not operate on ethnocentric assumptions about what a black student should be doing.
3. Distinguishing between valid learning difficulties and inappropriate expectations.

4. Being knowledgeable about the basis of an ethnic-
   sensitive practice.

Having set the educational and professional scene for practice
teaching, the following chapters set out the tasks, knowledge,
skills and techniques required for effective placement supervision.

2

Pre-placement Planning

The success of a placement will be enhanced by the amount of prior preparation by the practice teacher, the tutor and the student. Too often when supervisors meet together, one hears the familiar stories: hastily arranged, last minute placements; or students being disappointed that they couldn't get a preferred choice of placement or the aspect of a placement which they wanted. Clearly it is the course's responsibility to ensure that information on the variety of placements is available, and to suggest an appropriate placement to meet an individual student's learning needs. We would suggest, however, that poor planning on the part of the course is sometimes condoned by supervisors, who tend to act on the assumption that a preliminary request for a placement will automatically result in a placement being provided. In this chapter the issues that need to be considered in planning a placement will be introduced.

The process of placement planning proper starts when the prospective supervisor makes a commitment in principle to taking a student on placement. Even prior to that decision the social worker should have made a self-appraisal of his or her suitability to become a practice teacher. It is unlikely, unfortunately, that the teaching institution will see it as its responsibility to assess whether the prospective supervisor is ready to carry out the responsibilities of supervision. The only criterion that will probably be requested is that the supervisor has attended a student supervisors' course. The sole responsibility passes to the supervisor to decide whether he/she is ready. It can be a poor experience for a student, and the supervisor too, if the latter lacks confidence in his/her abilities and is made defensive or anxious by the demands of the role or by the challenge to his/her knowledge by taking on a student. Prospective supervisors can assume to be ready when they have established themselves in their practice role, and have sufficient confidence in their abilities overall to be able to admit to a lack of knowledge when this is experienced. They do not have to be omnicompetent. They should take the opportunity to discuss their intention with their line manager, who will have experience of a similar role and would be able to give them realistic feedback on their readiness. Attending a preparation course for prospective practice teachers will have provided further information on their aptitudes for this new role.

Following this personal appraisal, the next task is to produce a 'placement prospectus'. This involves an honest review of 'what's on offer', both in respect of work experiences which can be offered by the agency, and learning opportunities by the supervisor, such as special interests, knowledge and skills.

It is an important pre-requisite for the supervisor to understand that the student is on placement with the agency and supervised by the practice teacher, and not simply on placement with the supervisor. There are two issues here. First, if students are to experience fully the flavour of social work practice in the particular agency setting, they must have the same access to resources, personnel and knowledge about it as a staff member. They will not be able to do this if the agency has not endorsed their presence by a positively expressed wish to take students on placement. Second, part of the learning for students is to experience the opportunities and constraints of working in a particular agency. They need to learn how policies are formulated and expressed, how change is implemented, and the roles social workers take within the agency. They will also discover some of the normative values of the agency staff, particularly the views that senior personnel may hold about the appropriate expressions of the social worker's role. If students are to respond critically to this experience, and not be unthinkingly socialised by the viewpoints, ideas and opinions of others, then they will need to learn how to examine and analyse them.

Creating a profile of personal and agency resources

The following are suggested elements to be considered in a profile, whatever the agency setting. (The examples were produced by students on a supervisor training course, Leicester University School of Social Work, 1983.)

Description of the agency setting or the particular placement situation. What is the work setting? Is it a decentralised office? Would the student be working as a member of a team? How many team members are there? Are all team members social workers? Decentralised offices usually indicate a smaller work unit in which the ability of individuals to relate well to each other is important. There might be a particular team ethos to which temporary members of the team would be expected to subscribe. A student might find a small isolated work unit, with few colleagues available, unsupportive.

Example: the team thus comprises ten members and, because of its geographical spread and the nature of the area it serves (a distinct neighbourhood with a recognisable community identity) its members are all committed to working as a unified team.

The area covered by the agency. Information about the geography of the area is important: the size of the population, social mix, presence of a minority ethnic population, age structure of the population. The geography of the area raises questions as basic as whether a supervisor can accept a student who has no transport.

Example: (agency – probation) Typical inner-city area: 'red light' area; inner area development programme currently in operation. High itineracy; many clients living in lodging houses. High concentration of young offenders (17–25). Racial mix (Asian and Afro-Caribbean). Large proportion of women on probation as a result of laws on prostitution.

Brief profile of the supervisor. It is useful for the student to have a brief pen-picture of the supervisor's own experience to date, including particular skills available or knowledge about certain problems, for example, welfare rights, homelessness, marital counselling. The supervisor might have a special interest in a client group or be skilled in a particular method of intervention. It is even more useful to the student if supervisors can indicate their strengths – administration, for example – or their weaknesses – a tendency to be disorganised perhaps – or any particular idiosyncrasies, such as intolerance of laziness.

> **Example:** *I have worked for some seven years in residential child care working with adolescents in hostels in London, a CHE and at a children's centre. I have worked in my present office for two years; for eighteen months I was a member of a long-term team with a generic caseload with a weighting towards child care cases. For the past six months I have been a member of the duty team. As a supervisor I would see my main strengths as being an ability to enjoy the process of supervision, through examining motivation, responses and relationships. Also the stimulation of reassessing my own academic grasp of social work intervention.*

The range of students suitable for the placement. Here one would consider the experience of the student and possibly the ideological viewpoint held by the student. The less experienced supervisor is usually better working with a student of middle-range abilities to begin with, and with a student who has no known clear difficulties. A young, inexperienced student might find a prison or hospice setting stressful for a first placement. Substantial clashes of views between supervisor and student are probably best avoided.

> **Example: (day centre for recovering psychiatrically ill clients).** *Could be a placement for a much more experienced student who has a special interest in mental health work. Small staff group would have to limit supervision to a degree, but a student undertaking individual group therapy sessions would need to have already started to develop the appropriate skills.*

Social work methods that could be taught. Social work methods would range from the main approaches of group work, community work and casework, to more detailed specialisms such as behavioural casework, psychotherapy, task-centred casework, client-centred therapy and family therapy. The supervisor might offer a placement with an emphasis on psycho-drama, communicating with children through play, the use of sculpting in working with families, or of co-working in marital counselling. Supervisors should honestly assess whether they can really teach competently in relation to all the methods which they have set down.

Example: Casework, crisis intervention in the context of duty work; co-working; family therapy. Within the team: behavioural methods, group work, sculpting; fostering and adoption vetting.

Work and experience available. Included here are the learning experiences that can be offered to students through the types of problem referred to the agency, for example welfare rights work, or through the client groups, for example elderly or mentally ill clients. The supervisor should also consider the expertise available in the agency setting: the specialist workers such as court liaison officers, fostering workers or colleagues interested in women's issues.

Example: Long-term work available reflects the population of the area: a very high proportion of single parents and children under five, demanding a considerable input into preventive child care work. This often involves helping young, inexperienced parents, to cope with difficult behaviour problems and working jointly with health visitors in the area of child care education.

Methods for supervision and teaching which could be used. Here supervisors should make clear their expected style and methods of supervision including regularity of sessions, whether written work should be available to the supervisor before the session, or whether the supervisor will rely mainly on verbal accounts of work done. At a more technical level, reference should be made to methods of teaching which the supervisor anticipates using: video, tape-recorder, process recording, sitting in on interviews or using role play.

Example: (social services area team) Process recording, co-working, group supervision, group seminars and individual supervision.

The student as a resource to the placement. Students are valuable resources to agencies; they bring with them new knowledge and different points of view. In addition to the service they provide to clients, they might undertake small research or information-gathering projects, for example collating information on resources for elderly people in the area. Expectations of the role of the student within the team and the extent of the demands which would be made need to be clarified.

> **Example:** *A student could set up a series of sessions for a group of clients to supplement the range of activities normally on offer. This could be to teach a skill, for example, budget cookery, or to offer a particular therapy, for example, assertiveness exercises; or to focus on the special needs of a particular client group, for example, middle-aged widows.*

Other opportunities for learning. In order to maximise the learning for the student, the supervisor should look at other resources of personnel within the agency: colleagues in the team, specialist workers, other professionals within the agency.

> **Example:** *Opportunity exists for students to involve themselves in the day-to-day management and allocation of resources which are in the team, and to observe the management and committee structure of a local authority department.*

On a long placement it should be possible for the student, if desired, to undertake work in more than one part of the agency. It is important, however, that the overall supervision is carried out by the same practice teacher, so that the student's experience does not become that of brief separate placements.

Preparing a profile such as this completes the first stage of an appraisal of the supervisor's readiness to offer a placement. It has provided an opportunity to look at their new role as a student supervisor, perhaps for the first time.

The relationship between supervisor, student and tutor

A practice placement for a social work student involves a tripartite relationship between student, tutor and practice teacher. The relationship between tutor and practice teacher and the balance of responsibility and power between the two is not often considered. The basic requirements for this relationship, which are likely to see a placement through successfully, are:

1. An open, honest relationship between tutor and supervisor which has a sufficient degree of confidence in their respective abilities.
2. A genuine care and respect for the student by both.
3. A willingness to be open with each other in tripartite meetings with the student, even though, at times, any pair should feel able to discuss problems freely in the absence of the third party.

Supervisor's expectations of the tutor

In order to prepare for and plan the placement, supervisors need certain information from the tutor: about the course, about the student, and about the support they can expect from the tutor; and the supervisor should expect a pre-placement visit by the tutor to assess its suitability for the student.

The supervisor can expect to be provided with a course syllabus, which will include the chronology of the teaching inputs, so that the supervisor is able to perceive the student in the context of the total learning environment. The supervisor will need to know, for example, if any essays are to be completed during the placement and the dates of holidays so that work can be planned accordingly. Most courses provide guidelines to supervisors as to the content of the assessment report: the areas of work which should be assessed; the level of competence expected; and whether, in a longer placement, an interim report is required. If a placement is to involve a special project, it may be that the guidelines set are inappropriate, and supervisor, tutor and student will need to negotiate different ways of assessing the work.

The tutor can be expected to share with the supervisor (with the student's knowledge) information about the student's progress on the course. The supervisor needs a clear idea about the student's stage of professional development and what learning is hoped to be achieved on the placement. A frequent issue is whether or not a prospective supervisor should see previous placement reports. We have found it useful to view the total learning of the student, while on the course, as a continuum along which each teaching input and each practice placement takes the student some way. Supervisors must, therefore, have as much information as possible about the knowledge and skills that the student has so far acquired, and what gaps there might be, in order to plan their input and decide the possible learning tasks for the placement.

The tutor should have begun to prepare the student for the placement. This will have begun with discussions about types of placements in which the student is interested, e.g. a hospital, a social services area team, community social work, or day care setting. Further than this the student will have begun to formulate an understanding both of the learning possibilities in the placement they have chosen, e.g. adoption placement, and their individual learning goals, e.g. behavioural techniques, working with depressed clients or learning how to record appropriately.

Another important area for clarification at this stage of the planning is the amount of support the tutor can be expected to offer to the supervisor and to the placement generally. The tutor has a critical role in planning the placement, through being closely involved in working out the aims of the placement, the learning tasks, and being a party to the 'contract'. (We will be looking at 'contracts' in more detail in Chapter 3.)

The educational establishment might suggest a programme of three-way meetings which will provide the basis of contact between supervisor, student and tutor. The purpose of the meetings is to provide opportunities for evaluation of the students's progress. A format for these meetings might be: a description of the work undertaken by the student, the identification of learning opportunities, followed by an evaluation of achievement. If the supervisor is unable to provide the learning opportunities offered in the initial contract, this will need to be discussed with the tutor. In addition to these planned meetings, however, the supervisor should clarify with the tutor their availability and the best means of contact, should difficulties arise in the placement which warrant more immediate discussion. Further links between the educational establishment and the practice placement are often made through 'supervisors' meetings'. Through such meetings, supervisors can expect to be kept informed about current teaching on the course. These meetings also provide opportunities for discussion on the process of practice teaching, as well as aspects of social work education generally. Students may or may not be invited to such meetings.

Although educational establishments will usually reserve the right to take the final decision on whether or not a student has passed a placement, supervisors are expected to recommend a pass or fail. This is a legitimate expectation of a supervisor and is not a responsibility that should or can be shirked. The competent supervisor has a right to expect that his or her decision will be supported by the educational establishment. This is a responsibility with serious implications for the student and for future social work clients. It makes it very important that practice teachers are well prepared for their role and that they check very carefully the grounds on which the course will be asking them to evaluate their student's work.

Finally, supervisors have the right to expect that students are adequately prepared by their tutors for placement. Occasionally, because of the tight timetabling of teaching and practice components of a course, on the first day of a placement a supervisor might find that a student is emotionally drained, because the deadline for a written assignment was the previous day.

Preparation by the student for the placement

At a minimum, students should know in principle what it is they are required to know by the end of the course. This is regarded as the learning '*curriculum*': students progress along *a continuum* towards this goal as they acquire knowledge and develop skills. In planning for the placement, students should have some idea of their development in relation to the curriculum, and can, therefore, be expected to be able to state their broad aims for any placement.

Learning tasks for the student

Before considering the aims of any particular placement, it is necessary to look at the overall learning tasks of the social work student in the process of becoming a knowledgeable and skilled practitioner.

Social work is a complex activity requiring a large range of knowledge, which must be applied in a discriminating fashion to unique, personal situations in an individualised way by the practitioner. It is understandable that the social work student may at first feel that the knowledge required is impossible to encompass; indeed, it is one of the reasons why the profession continues to be partialised by agency setting and, increasingly, by specialisms within them.

However, in our view Lewis (1972) offers a very useful framework which student and supervisor can use to unravel the complex knowledge needed. Lewis argues that there are three main kinds of knowledge which the social worker uses: values, theory and practice. These are utilised in relation to those important practical concerns of the social worker, namely agency function, the problem to be tackled, and the process of intervention. When these three aspects of knowledge are cross-related to the three demands of social work concern, they produce nine types of knowledge, which are both universal to all social work situations and comprehensive in their coverage. Lewis displays the categories usefully in the form of a table (see next page).

The concerns of social work are limited to these categories of knowledge; when the supervisor and student address the case, problem, project or situation at hand, both the factors which go to make up the problem situation and the knowledge which informs the problem and the intervention can be

	Values	*Knowledge*	*Practice*
Agency function	Policy	Theory	Task
Problem	Problem condition	Proposition (how)	Role
Process	Ethical Imperatives	Methods Techniques Skills	Relationship

fitted into the framework of categories provided. It goes without saying that the combination of unique factors and knowledge requirements for any single intervention multiplied by the variety of problem conditions, explanations for them, agency provision, methods of intervention, etc., go to make up a lifetime of learning for the average social worker.

Acquiring skills. Towle (1954) maintained that there were no skills in social work beyond the ability to use knowledge in helping people. However, using knowledge to help people requires a multiplicity of skills, from basic practice skills – for example the ability to listen and manage face-to-face contact with people – to being skilled in specific methods of intervention – for example behaviour modification or family therapy. Below are listed a number of skills that were suggested by potential student supervisors on our preparation course in 1983:
1. Interviewing techniques.
2. The ability to collect data.
3. Skills in assessing needs of clients and how to go about meeting those needs.
4. Skills in diplomacy.
5. The ability to make decisions.
6. Skill in recording and report writing.
7. Administrative skills in managing a workload.
8. The ability to acquire resources to meet a client's needs.
9. Skill in evaluating intervention.

Methods of social work. Supervisors share responsibility in ensuring that newly qualified social workers have knowledge and skills in a range of interventive methods which they draw on to use according to the problem. Students on our supervisors' courses included the following:

1. Casework: counselling, task-centred work, crisis intervention.
2. Group work: skill in running therapy groups, encouraging self-help groups.
3. Community social work.

Role of the social worker. Students are acquiring a professional role which has to be compatible with their sense of self, their values and attitudes. Part of this identity will be gained through contact with other people in the role, with whom they will want to identify to a greater or lesser degree. Students have to develop their own way of offering their social work skills, in the context of a recognisable job, so that they can be used with discrimination in relation to a variety of problem situations with which they will be faced. They have to learn the limitations and boundaries of the profession, and how to relate in a professional way to clients, colleagues and other professionals.

Knowledge of self. Students have to develop self-awareness, recognition of their own values and attitudes, knowledge of their strengths and weaknesses, and how to apply personal experience to the work.

Functions and tasks of the agency. Finally, students are learning about the functions and tasks of the agency in which they are placed. This will include local knowledge of the area and the resources available within the community.

The above constitutes a learning curriculum for any social work student. What, then, is the function of the practice placement?

Aims and expectations of the placement for the student

An essential element in social work education and training is the experience that students obtain through supervised social work practice. Practice placements provide opportunities for students to test their suitability for social work; their capacity to give service, by offering opportunities to become involved in helping clients. Over recent years, the average age of entrants into social work qualifying courses has decreased, so that many students have little experience of statutory social services before starting a course. But the process in which students are involved in testing themselves as practitioners is not a simple matter. Practice placements offer opportunities to develop a large number and wide range of skills, and they also provide a complex context for learning in which the student is provided with numerous learning opportunities, receives extensive teaching, and is required to reach an adequate standard of overall performance.

Practice placements are usually provided in a team setting, so that the student is able to learn not only about the agency, its resources and how it achieves its tasks, but also about the functioning of a small work unit. The student develops as a team member, using colleagues as models and all the time evolving an independent perspective on the role of social worker. Students are free to explore their own ideas, discover their own 'truths' and their way of doing social work. Hopefully, the supervisor is a facilitator in this process.

Establishing the learning tasks of the placement

With a knowledge of what the student has to learn to become a skilled practitioner and an understanding of how the practice placement fits into the overall pattern, it should not be difficult to establish what the student might expect, and be expected, to learn in a placement.

Students often have clear ideas on the type of placement they are seeking and will specify a particular agency or even a particular supervisor. However, when it comes to discussing more precisely what they expect to learn on the placement, students sometimes appear confused by the nature of the question: they make vague comments about work with particular client groups, or conversely have very definite ideas on methods of working which they want to learn or explore in more depth.

It is unacceptable for students to begin negotiations for placements without much thought about where they are in terms of their professional development and, as discussed earlier, a supervisor should expect that part of the tutor's role is to prepare their students for the placement. We suggest that this should include discussion of the student's learning needs and expectations of the placement. If insufficient preparation has been done by the tutor and student, a supervisor is justified in suggesting that more thought should be given to the placement before their next meeting.

Other sources of information

The supervisor has available other sources of information to gauge the student's progress on the 'learning continuum'. The tutor will usually have provided a curriculum vitae on the student, detailing previous work experience, voluntary work experience, education, interests, etc. Previous placement reports should be available to the new supervisor, and from the course syllabus it should be possible to see what subjects have been taught so far. Bertha Reynolds (1965), in her concept of the learning continuum, describes various stages of development and the student's response:
(a) Acute self-consciousness
(b) Sink or swim adaptation
(c) Understanding, but without the ability to put all of it into action
(d) Relative mastery
We often see these stages illustrated in our own experience, for example being thrown in at the deep end, or where students feel that they have worked more effectively before they started training.

Further considerations

Although the establishment of a student's learning needs is fundamental to planning a placement, consideration should also be given to the student's particular interests, which may be explored during a placement. A limitation on the extent to which a student's needs can be met on any placement is what the supervisor can offer. However much goodwill there is on the supervisor's part, and however much pressure there is from the educational establishment to accept the student, it would be wrong to accept a student whose needs the supervisor cannot meet, for example because of unavailability of appropriate learning opportunities.

Pre-placement planning within the agency

If the tutor has responsibility for preparing a student for placement, then the prospective supervisor has the clear responsibility for preparing the 'agency', whatever the setting, for the student. (More detailed suggestions covering the period immediately prior to the student's arrival are given in Chapter 4.) Until recently, social work agencies had a vested interest in offering practice placements to students: an agency which offered satisfactory placements attracted newly qualified practitioners at a time when the recruitment of qualified staff was often difficult. In the present employment climate, with many qualified social workers chasing fewer vacancies, there is no longer the pressure to offer placements as a means of recruitment. Few agencies have ever offered material incentives to their student supervisors, nor, apparently, have they valued supervisors' contribution to perpetuating the profession by making space within workloads for the added responsibilities. Nevertheless, practitioners seem to have considered this final stage in the development of their professional role, that of teaching the art that they have accomplished, to be a natural progression. Even now there still appears to be a steady clamour for preparation courses for student supervision.

As stated earlier, a student is on placement with the agency, and ideally the status of practice supervisor is one that should be recognised, supported and valued by the agency if the student is to benefit fully from the placement. Although the agency as a whole might be ambivalent in its policy on offering practice placements, the supervisor must ensure that the immediate team or staff group with whom the student will work has a positive commitment to taking students. Particular teams or settings may receive too many requests for placements, and it may be necessary to 'ration' placements or work a rota of supervisors. Few supervisors are in a position to agree to take a student without first negotiating with colleagues and establishing whether or not they have agreement. Individual supervisors' needs have to be considered *vis-à-vis* the agency/area/team's needs and ability to take students.

The potential supervisor needs to establish some basic ground rules with colleagues:

1. That there is agreement that the placement is to proceed and that colleagues will be supportive towards the supervisor. The student not only directly increases the workload of the supervisor, but indirectly ensures that other colleagues will have to take additional work which the supervisor is unable to do.

2. That colleagues will participate in providing learning opportunities for students, from taking them on observation visits, to possibly supervising a particular piece of work in which they have a specialised skill to offer.

3. It is important to establish the status of the student while on the placement. Will the student have the status of a full team member as far as attending team meetings or training sessions is concerned? How will work be selected for the student: at normal allocation meetings, or will the supervisor be allowed to select appropriate work for the student prior to the allocation meeting? The student will want to be clear as to what decisions can be taken without confirmation by the supervisor or more senior personnel.

4. At this stage of planning, the supervisor may decide it is appropriate to discuss where the student will actually sit. Which room and with which colleagues will the student be placed? Is there another student in the agency and should they sit together for mutual support? A great deal of informal learning is achieved as the student sits in the office observing the attitudes of colleagues – the way they talk on the telephone and in office discussions. Colleagues who share rooms with students need to be prepared for this voyeurism.

Conclusions

1. We suggest that it is useful to look at a student's learning in terms of a continuum. A supervisor needs to know how far the student has progressed already in order that the learning aims for a particular placement can be planned. It is important to do this so that teaching is appropriate to the student's abilities and it also helps to avoid duplication of teaching on placements. It follows, therefore, that there is little validity in the attitude occasionally expressed by supervisors that to know too much about a student's previous placement(s) will prejudice their own attitude. It is not fair either to the students or to supervisors themselves to assume that they might be easily influenced by tutors or previous supervisors.
2. Supervision is a responsibility that quite rightly demands effort by the supervisor in terms of preparation. Students and their tutors have a right to expect that a prospective supervisor will have clear, well thought-out ideas as to what is on offer in the placement.
3. Prospective supervisors have a responsibility to say 'no' if they are not confident that theirs is the right placement for the student or that this is the right student for the placement.
4. Practice placements play a primary role in the education and training of student social workers, and supervisors should expect that tutors will visit the placement to assess its suitability for their students.
5. Supervisors must play an active part in negotiating placements. They have a right to as much information as possible on the student. A placement should not go ahead until a 'contract' is reached, and discussions may need several meetings. We look at 'contracts' in more detail in Chapter 3.

3

Contract Making

The aim of this chapter is to examine the process of negotiating a contract with the student, to offer suggestions about the content of the contract, and to explore the importance of the contract as an anchor to the whole placement.

In recent years there has been a growth in interest in contract making in social work intervention, through approaches such as task-centred casework and problem-solving (Reid and Epstein, 1972, 1977). These approaches emphasise the responsibility on the part of the client to co-operate freely with the social worker, thus forging a partnership, with shared responsibility for the tasks that must be undertaken. The client's motivation is enhanced by a willingness to work on problems that are personally relevant and especially where there is agreement on the goals to be achieved and on the methods of reaching them. Although there is a degree of dependency in problem-solving as there is in any learning, clients are not helpless; they should be able to recognise their own needs, and able to take a considerable share of the responsibility for meeting them.

In social work education and training the 'contract', or 'compact' as some would prefer, is a specific and explicit way of identifying the expectations between the student and the supervisor which will govern the learning opportunities in the placement (Parsloe, 1978; Robinson, 1978; Thomas and Tierney, 1982). The expectations which make up the contract between the student, practice teacher and tutor, will be of three kinds:
1. implicit;
2. of a general nature arising out of the course itself;

3. special or particular expectations arising out of the nature of the placement.

Implicit expectations. There is a level of expectations held by the parties involved which would not be spelled out in the course of making a contract for a placement, and about which it would be unreasonable to complain if they were included in the contract. They are not simply the rules of common sense, common courtesy or the ordinary expectations of commonplace relationships in working life. Those are important, of course, and include such things as the student keeping agreed office hours punctually or the supervisor turning up to supervisory meetings which have been agreed. The basic, implicit assumptions about students are that they are motivated to undertake the placement and that they are educable for social work. This would not be questioned during the contract-making exercise unless these aspects had been called into question by earlier experiences. Similarly, it is implicitly assumed that supervisors are competent in practice and supervision, and a contrary judgement would have to be proved through the experience of a placement. Again, it would be the implicit expectation of an agency that it was prepared to accept the student, and to make its facilities available in the same way as for other employees.

Any social work placement is first and foremost with the agency and not with the particular supervisor. For each placement the supervisor is assigned by the agency to conduct (a) the practice on behalf of the agency, and (b) the training on behalf of the course, and both are brought together in the role of the practice teacher. It is implicit, then, that both parties will conduct themselves in ways which do not have to be spoken about, unless they should prove a problem.

Course expectations. The most general expectation that a social work course has about a placement is that it is relevant to the role of a social worker. Furthermore, it is expected that the work assigned to the student throughout the placement will be pertinent to the skills to be learned. Lastly, it is expected that the student will be comprehensively assessed on all the aspects of practice which make up the social worker role.

Not all activity which is helpful to people is necessarily that which should be undertaken by a social worker. A good test for the relevance of a particular agency for the placement of a student is whether that agency ordinarily employs a qualified social worker to tackle the problems involved and to undertake the tasks which are entailed. In general it is not appropriate to experiment with the welfare of social work students by placing them in settings where the relevance of the work is in doubt. Quite properly there is constant innovation in social work, seeking out new areas of need and experimenting with new methods of intervention, but students' training experience is too short, and the risks of a worthless placement too great, for experimentation to be justified at this stage in their development. Similarly, not all the work that is undertaken within an agency is appropriate to be undertaken by social workers, and care needs to be taken that a student is not misused as a general dogsbody, or assigned duties that are not relevant to the job of learning to become a social work practitioner. Research, management, teaching and administration are all specialisms which social workers undertake at later stages in their professional development, but it is inappropriate for any of these functions to become a primary task of students during the period of their basic training. It is in the nature of training that competence has not yet been demonstrated, and all social work courses need to decide whether their students have reached an adequate standard in order to be approved as qualified to enter the profession. It is the duty of a social work course to formulate the criteria according to which the performance will be judged and to assess what is reasonable in terms of expectations.

The particular placement. As we mentioned earlier, social work is provided within an institutional context in Britain, and many of these settings are characterised by particular problems, age populations, or methods of intervention. While social workers are generically trained, they choose to work in particular agency settings throughout their career.

Similarly, the initial career opportunities of social work students will be shaped by the agency placement choices they make.

Some examples of contracts made for placements

The following are extracts from actual contracts made between supervisors, tutors and students, for various kinds of placements and at different stages throughout a course. The contract is frequently prepared and written by the tutor, as this seems to be a common expectation, but it will have arisen out of preplacement discussions between the tutor and the student, and then between all three participants together.

Example A

This is a contract for a first placement for a student entering a voluntary agency with a responsibility for helping families, but with staff who specialise in brief approaches to family therapy. An extract only is provided in order to protect the anonymity of the placement. The student has had considerable experience of practice as a social worker in a social services department prior to the course.

Broad aims
1. To learn the theory and practice of brief therapy and the issues arising from the application of theory to social work clients.
2. To evaluate Sarah's basic skills in interviewing and assessment.
3. To assist in identifying those skills which Sarah already possesses by virtue of her previous experiences.

Description of workload
1. *Hours.* Comparable to full-time workers with time off in lieu for evening and extra work.
2. *General description of the work.* Learning the theoretical perspective and observation for the first three weeks; then interviews with live consultation. It may not be possible within the time allocated for Sarah to complete a case.
3. *Client or target groups.* Individuals or pairs of clients referred either by social services or by themselves.

4. *Methods of work*. Brief therapy.
Supervision
1. *Timetabling of sessions*. Weekly, 1½ hours.
2. *Assessment methods*. Observation and live consultation. One to one supervision. Video analysis of interviews. Examination of theoretical text.
3. *Assessment framework*. The School's practice guide.
Student's accommodation
Desk in a shared office.
Role of tutor
1. To identify the learning issues relevant to Sarah's professional development.
2. To check that the assessment process is running smoothly.
Tutorial visits
1. *Frequency*. Three visits in total.
2. *Agenda*. All three of us to come with a planned agenda.

Example B

This contract relates to a main placement in a community social work 'patch' office where the student is planning to make her career in social services fieldwork. The student already has considerable experience of social services area team work.

Marilyn's second and main placement is located in a social services neighbourhood centre, which uses a social network approach to helping people in need in the local community. A preplacement visit has been undertaken and a very thorough outline of the practice and learning opportunities available has been discussed. No firm decisions were made at that meeting as to the kind of work which Marilyn will undertake. She will decide finally in the first two weeks of the placement, which will be devoted primarily to learning the routines of the office and providing a welfare rights service to residents who come to the centre.

A welfare rights take-up campaign will be operating in the neighbourhood throughout June, and the workers at the centre will be involved in a follow-up over the next four weeks and it is likely that Marilyn will be involved in that work. The centre is also going to be a part of a housing action area which will involve improvements in housing for occupiers and the amenities in the area generally.

Other projects which will be available to Marilyn are as follows:
 (i) Four morning advice and counselling sessions, for people who come to the centre, which may involve some individual work and follow up at home.
 (ii) Possibly setting up a claimants unit, which Marilyn is interested in and which may arise out of welfare rights take-up campaign.
 (iii) A district heating scheme action group, to examine deficiencies in the scheme before winter comes on, and where people no longer get their heating additions.
 (iv) The tenants' association, which involves a lot of informal contact with people living in the area.
 (v) The area review board; a group of professionals and residents involved in the area.
 (vi) A community newspaper which has a new editor and the project may have a role in supporting it.
 (vii) A volunteer network, e.g. street warden scheme.
 (viii) Indirect approaches, e.g. the development of other natural helping networks within the community.

Example C

This contract relates to a main placement in a probation area team, where the student is intending to take up a career with the probation service. The student has no prior experience of probation work, but prior to the course spent one year working in a probation hostel as an assistant warden. His first placement was in a community work setting, working on behalf of homeless young people.

Tom's central concern in coming to his main probation placement is that he should gain a broad experience of the duties of a main grade probation officer. Within those duties he would like a great variety of need, age range, problems, etc., so that he maximises the range of his learning. In the preplacement meeting it was agreed that the placement would attempt to achieve this as far as possible. It was noted that the probation service is currently engaged in a review of its priorities following the recent Home Office report, and there is likely to be a new emphasis on involving the community in supporting the work of the service. [The supervisor] intends to provide Tom with a broad induction experience into the general work of the agency, through joint visits, e.g. to a prison to meet a life sentence prisoner, spending a day with community service, and perhaps a period at the day centre, although this is not fully operational at the moment. Within the broad range of learning opportunities which Tom would like to gain, he also has particular interests in marriage counselling, divorce court welfare, working with sexual offenders and with women clients. There is a possibility of undertaking some marital work, perhaps jointly with another worker, later in the placement.

It was noted that Tom has a case study to undertake during the period of the placement, but this will be his responsibility, although naturally the work will be supervised. We discussed the methods of teaching and learning, and we hope that they would extend beyond the discussion method or teaching from case records, with a possibility of sitting in on Tom's interviews and the use of audio.

Example D

This is a main placement in a voluntary agency specialising in placing difficult-to-place children with families. The student is an experienced residential social worker who intends to return to residential care on completion of the course. She undertook her first placement in a social services department area team.

In wishing to undertake the placement with [project] Linda is making a very specialised choice of experience and one in which she has high motivation to learn and to give service. She is aware of the changing trends in ideas about the care of children and sees this aspect of work as very relevant to her professional needs, both in returning to her residential work following the course and even if she becomes a field social worker. As a result of the preplacement meeting which we undertook, we felt a viable placement emerged, in which Linda could have the opportunity to undertake the following kinds of work. The possibility of becoming involved in developing publicity on some of the children that the agency wished to place with foster parents. There is likely to be a series of preparation meetings for applicants in the autumn; the format is one which is of great interest to Linda, and in which she would be very pleased to participate. She would like an opportunity to become involved in, and to take responsibility for, the assessment process for individual applicants.

Issues to be taken into account by the supervisor

The supervisor is the party to the contract who is ultimately responsible for ensuring that the contract is properly negotiated and agreed on a competent basis. The reason for this is that supervisors are usually both more experienced generally in social work and more knowledgeable about the agency setting. Thus they can be expected to have the knowledge from which to (a) cover their side of a competent contract, and (b) ensure that the student's side of a contract is properly protected and to be prepared to do this on their behalf if necessary. This does not mean that students should be viewed as helpless, dependent or ineffectual people, as many of them will be prepared, thoughtful and able to argue for their own interests. In addition, the tutor and the course staff have a responsibility to play their part in preparing students for the placement, and thus to ensure that they are sufficiently knowledgeable to engage in negotiating in a responsible and effective way. However, it is the supervisor who is finally responsible for ensuring that the process of the negotiation is handled properly and that the final contract is meaningful, in the sense that it is properly understood and agreed to by the student. In the last resort, if an inadequate contract is agreed to, then an examination of the reasons for this should properly begin with the supervisor.

The process of contract making

The making of a contract between the supervisor and the student begins prior to the placement. Final agreement on a placement should be subject to a contract being completed. In general, the content of a contract will comprise:
1. The work that is to be undertaken by the student, e.g. types of cases to be assigned, the particular responsibilities in the residential setting, or the type of project in a community work agency.
2. The learning needs of the student, which will include the tasks to be undertaken in the agency, the social work skills

to be acquired, and any particular learning difficulties that are to be overcome.

3. The teaching/learning methods of the placement, through which the supervision will be conducted.

4. The 'conditions of service' of the placement, e.g. hours of work, time-keeping, use of a car, etc.

It is these aspects which have to be negotiated and agreed. One issue that is often raised at this stage of placement planning is whether the previous placement report should be seen by the next supervisor. The argument can range from withholding it in principle, to an insistence that it should be seen in every instance. Those who object to the report being sent on argue that it can label the student and prevent the next supervisor from seeing the student and their work through fresh eyes. Those in favour of the report being seen argue that learning is a continuum, and that it is facilitated in the next placement by the supervisor being made aware, at an early stage, of the nature and strengths and weaknesses of the previous learning by the student.

We take the view that it makes placement reports rather pointless if they are not passed on to the next supervisor; the training part of a course should be seen as a whole learning process, with each supervisor doing their part in the interests of the student's total learning needs. We would go as far as to say that a supervisor should seriously question the assumptions about the coming placement if sight of the report is refused. It must be remembered that placement reports belong to the course and not to the student, and as long as the report has been competently written, then the next supervisor should be able to read it. Otherwise the supervisor is dependent on a second-hand account of the earlier placement, which seems unnecessary and overprotective. Also, the report gives the practice teacher important clues as to the kind of supervision the student had previously. The only circumstances in which a course's staff should consider withholding the earlier report is where their misgivings about the content is such that it calls the report's validity into question.

Having the report does raise problems about labelling the student. Perhaps a problem exhibited in an earlier placement was not as prominent as the first supervisor believed; or perhaps it has been given greater weight by being put into writing; or perhaps it has been overcome and is not likely to reappear unless it is magnified by the expectations of the new supervisor. Despite these possible objections, we believe that it is essential for the report to be provided. In our view, supervisors are people who, cognisant of a student's problems, will not necessarily assume that the problem will resurface in the coming placement. However, if an earlier difficulty does present itself again, then not to have the report means that the supervisor has to start from scratch, wasting time needlessly, and forgoing the help of the previous supervisor. It will be necessary to identify and discuss any objections which the student has to the content of the report, so that they are fully and sympathetically understood. The difficulties can then be set aside in their full knowledge, in the context of the new opportunities and challenges of the coming placement.

We shall now look in more detail at each aspect of the content of the contract: the work, learning needs, the teaching/learning methods, and the conditions of the placement.

Work tasks and methods

The primary task for the student in a placement is not, as it is for ordinary employees, to give service to clients, but to *learn how* to give service. Thus the primary focus is to provide the conditions in which that learning can take place, so that by the end of a course a student is able to reach the standard from which it can be reasonably predicted that he or she will provide an adequate level of service in a future full-time job. The work or learning tasks for a student in a placement involve:
1. learning about the services which clients need;
2. learning to assess people's needs in relation to those services;
3. learning the methods of giving those services;
4. transferring that learning appropriately to other, similar situations;

5. acquiring the general role of a social worker and learning how to apply it differentially to varying problems, needs and population groups.

The nature of work differs depending on the placement setting, and thus it is more useful to refer to it as work tasks or workloads rather than the traditional notion of caseloads. Work may take the form of cases which are assigned in a fieldwork setting; or tasks such as getting children up in the morning in a residential setting; teaching a handicapped person new life skills; or planning and implementing a neighbourhood project in a community work setting. Whatever the nature of the work assigned, it should share the following characteristics:

1. The student should have a clear, independent, participative role. Observation placements are not appropriate for social workers in training.
2. The student should have a clearly defined responsibility to carry out the particular task, even if that responsibility is shared in a collective effort with other members of the team.
3. It should be possible to be individually accountable for something which is both measurable and has a definite outcome.
4. It should be work which is characteristically carried out by a social worker and is complex work requiring the exercise of planning, discretion and judgement for it to be completed successfully.

We said earlier that the learning task for the student involved the acquisition of the knowledge and skills of the generic social work role, as well as the special inputs of the particular setting. The placement provides an opportunity to apply the knowledge and to practise skills in a relatively protected and supportive setting. Depending on the placement, the emphasis of the method may well be in practice with individuals, group work, residential social work or community work. The aim for the student will be to acquire the knowledge and skills of the process of intervention within those methods. In addition, the student comes to the particular setting in order to learn about the needs of particular client groups, e.g. mentally handicapped adults, economically deprived fam-

ilies, terminally ill patients, or people suffering from dilapi-
dated housing or poor environmental facilities. One possible
motivation for learning about the particular difficulties facing
clients might be to lay the foundations for a future career in an
occupational specialism such as probation. Finally, the
student will be coming to learn the knowledge and skills of
indirect work with clients. This will involve learning to work
within the opportunities and constraints of an agency setting;
working with members of a team; perhaps working with
members of other professional disciplines; and also learning
to work with members of other organisations.

The individual learning needs of the student

It goes without saying that all social work students are
different and thus they will learn differently and express their
social worker role in different ways. They will each develop
an individual style of working based on gender, class,
personal experiences, education, and pre-course and within-
course learning experiences. Hopefully, their professional
performance will have more similarities than differences as a
result of the education and training they receive. But they will
have different learning needs beyond the generic knowledge
and skills and the special interests in the placement.

Students will need to learn about the strengths and
limitations of their own style of doing social work, and these
will emerge in relation to the work they undertake with
particular problems, needs and tasks.

Some of their learning expectations will reflect the stage of
the student's learning within the course itself. A first placement student will have different expectations to one in a main
or final placement. Learning is a continuing process, both
within the course and in relation to the student's experience
prior to it.

However, beyond these considerations, a student may
have additional and special learning needs. They may be of
three kinds:
1. Learning situations which, in anticipation, cause the
   student worry. They may have arisen within the course,
   e.g. role-playing interviewing skills; within their pre-

course experience, e.g. dealing with aggressive people; or within their personal life, e.g. keeping appointments, punctuality, etc.
2. Learning problems which have been identified in earlier placements. They may take the form of specific aspects of performance, e.g. the ability to record work regularly and economically. They will need to be focused on in a constructive way, talked about, learned and practised again within the job.
3. Exceptional learning desires, arising out of cultural, political or biographical factors, for example: black students might need to learn to cope with the racism of white clients and white institutions; women might need to learn a feminist approach to helping when dealing with sexist colleagues, clients and institutions; and handicapped students might need to adapt their disabilities and to test them for a full professional role.

Teaching/learning methods

Teaching/learning methods are the ways in which the supervisor gains access to the performance and learning of the student, and they provide much of the content of discussion in the supervision sessions. They will be examined in detail in Chapters 6 and 7. They are the substance of the supervisor's side of the contract, and the ideas about them will normally be initiated by the supervisor. However, some students may have suggestions themselves, e.g. the use of audio recording, and there may be some methods the prospect of which makes them uneasy. However, the discussion should go beyond simply the methods themselves, and include the supervisor's general approach and even philosophy if he or she has one.

The supervisor's general approach to supervision may be deeply influenced by his/her approach to social work in general or by the demands of the setting in which the placement is located. For example, it may be difficult for a supervisor to work outside a behavioural approach to problems and this may require a student to work within that discipline. The whole approach of a team in a residential setting may be influenced in a similar way. This would need to be made explicit during the negotiation of the contract. In general, there is likely to be a congruence between the style and content of supervision and the style and content of the work between the student and client.

If a supervisor has a general philosophy or coherent set of expectations towards his/her supervisory style, then it would be best to explain this to the student at this stage. For example, a supervisor may expect a student to follow the particular ethos in a residential centre, so that there is consistency for clients, but indicate that anything about the work can be challenged and discussed in supervision sessions. In a community work project it may have been found that a community action approach works best and it may not be possible for a student to negotiate outside that model.

Beyond that, a supervisor may have expectations of specific teaching/learning methods which will be a part of the placement. The supervisor will need to indicate the range of the teaching/learning methods available, those about which the student has no choice, and those about which preferences can be negotiated. The frequency of supervision will be established, as well as the regular, routine requirements that will make up the pattern of the placement, for instance that records will be written up before discussion, and that the supervisor will expect to sit in on some of the student's interviews, require the student to undertake a process recording, and will ask colleagues how they are finding the student. There should be agreement regarding arrangements for informal discussions with the supervisor or with other colleagues, and the requirements of the supervision itself.

The organisation of the placement

Settings vary in their conditions of employment, because these are often shaped by the service needs of client groups as well as by the more informal practices which grow up. By and large students are expected to fit in with those practices, although as they are not full-time employees, they are not expected to meet the usual conditions of employment where these involve additional duties.

It will be the responsibility of the supervisor to explain the normal working hours in the agency, the arrangements for time off in lieu for out-of-hours work and the expectations with regard to evening work. In a residential placement, work will be organised through a pattern of shifts, and special arrangements may need to be made for a student, in order to facilitate their special learning role, or to ensure that they are able to work regularly with particular people. The supervisor must decide whether a student is to 'live in' or, where this is not possible or required, to undertake some overnight shifts in order to experience late-night and early-morning work. Increasingly, residential work does not mean that staff are resident, only that the clients are.

Arrangements may be made to allow for some formal study time for the student; certainly enough time needs to be set aside for a student to prepare for supervision, recognising the primary task of learning. In some placements it is crucial that the student can travel regularly and flexibly, and it may be necessary for the student to be able to drive or to have their own transport available.

4

Setting the Scene for Learning

There is an important period of time for the supervisor between completing the contract negotiations and thus making a commitment to the placement, and the day when the student actually arrives to begin the placement. We have called the work that should be undertaken during this period 'setting the scene for learning'. This is the final opportunity for the supervisor to complete the necessary preparations for the smooth induction of the student into the placement and to provide the basis for a sound learning experience. This period may be as long as two months or more, but it may also be as short as only a few weeks. It is an opportunity to implement the commitments in principle which have led to the offer of the placement in the first place. Understandably, until the decision to take a particular student is made, the idea of a placement is a rather abstract one. The decision now has real implications, and the success or otherwise of the preparations for the placement will certainly affect the welfare of the student in the early stages. It may have a lasting influence throughout the placement.

In setting the scene for learning in the placement, the practice teacher is undertaking this on behalf of the agency, the student, the tutor and the supervision. The impact of first impressions may not be sufficiently great to make or break a placement, but it can set it off on the wrong basis. It can sometimes be difficult for a placement to recover from a poor early start, and it is a pity to let this happen by default, as it is unnecessary and can be avoided. We examine the implications of this stage of planning for the placement from the

47

perspective of all the parties involved. Understandably, we begin with the practice teacher, because this is the person who has the responsibility for initiating, implementing and monitoring the planning.

The practice teacher

A first consideration for the supervisor should be to plan a reduction in his/her other workload responsibilities in order to take account of the time and energy demands of the new role. This should begin immediately, as the duties start well before the student arrives. Agreement to this in principle should have been a part of the decision to take a student in the first place and would have been taken more fully into account at the stage of contract negotiation. Now is the time to begin to implement it. The supervisor not only needs to reduce his/her workload for the duration of the placement, but it would also be helpful to plan for free time during the first week of the placement, as this is likely to be an intensive period of additional responsibilities. It is helpful if the student is organised into the general structure of the supervisor's work responsibilities. The student represents an assignment of 'work' for the duration of the placement, not an addition to normal responsibilities. The experience of many practice teachers might suggest that this is an unrealistic expectation in many agencies, where workloads are high and little or no allowance is made for taking students. This is undoubtedly the case in many instances, but representations can and should be made for an allowance in workload if the student (and the supervisor) is to experience a fair deal.

The supervisor should plan to be available for the first few days of the placement, not on a continuous basis, but recognising that the student is likely to need to consult frequently during the process of settling in. Otherwise, other staff will have to fulfil that role, which may be irksome, more time-consuming, and may lead to misunderstandings. It is a period of information-giving to the student and of introductions, and there may well be unforeseen contingencies. Although the supervisor will not be able to anticipate every eventuality, he or she can plan to be available, and this will be appreciated by the student.

Nearer to the time of arrival, the supervisor should start to plan in detail the work tasks that are going to be assigned to the student. It is important that these should be conveyed to the student in a thoughtful, unhurried way, and this requires an opportunity to study the work tasks and to consider the implications for the particular student. When the student arrives it will be necessary to reiterate the form of the placement to the student, as a reminder of the discussions which took place during the contract stage. Planning which takes into account the work that the student will undertake is a very important aspect at this stage. After all, it is the main means by which the student will learn during the placement and will be high on his or her agenda of priorities. Lastly, supervisors may find it useful to meditate a little on the prospect before them, by thinking back to the time when they were students, particularly at this stage of their placements. It can provide an opportunity to empathise with the likely feelings of the student, thus providing a basis for rapport between them.

The agency

We have continually emphasised the importance of the institutional setting in social work in the form of the agency, and at this stage, in this context, planning takes on three aspects:
— the immediate team colleagues
— the administration of the agency
— the facilities available to a student

Immediate colleagues

Colleagues must be informed of the expected arrival of the student. It is a reminder of their original commitment to help to provide a constructive learning experience for the student. The quality of the placement will depend in part on them. Some current experience of placements suggests that the constructive participation of other colleagues is very high, and supervisors consistently rate their contribution to students' learning very positively (Leicester University School of Social Work, 1984). Nearer to the time of starting it would be helpful to remind them of appropriate personal and professional details about the new student colleague, and to ask them if they will be available on the first day, so that the student can be introduced. Some of them may need reminding that they have agreed to participate in the student's induction programme.

Administration

Willingness to prepare the members of the administration of the agency emphasises that the student becomes a part of the agency organisation. The members of the administration who are likely to be involved with the student should be sent the same details as team colleagues. Closer to the time it will be necessary to inform those responsible for records, travelling expenses, car loan insurance, etc. The switchboard operator is a key person to be informed. Depending on the placement, there may be keys to be allocated, security to be cleared, the Official Secrets Act to be signed, and other formal procedures or informal matters to be facilitated.

In settings such as residential and day care, where clients are an ever-present part of the organisation, and indeed of the management, they also need to be prepared for the new arrival. They may well have been consulted in the original decision to take a student.

The student's personal facilities

Good facilities cannot compensate for a poor quality learning experience, but it is a romantic notion that students can put up with anything as long as they are in a good learning situation. The quality of the facilities is part of the enhancement of learning for the student and will certainly have an effect on performance. The aim should be to achieve a standard similar to that for other social workers in the agency, at least for block placements: a desk to work on, a room if possible, and a telephone; if not a separate room, then somewhere to study in preparation for supervision. A file of agency memoranda and forms shows attention to detail, and access to a dictaphone is helpful. If the agency has a handbook of working procedures, this can be helpful for a student to study at the beginning of a placement, and can save a supervisor considerable time which might otherwise be taken up with lengthy explanations. The provision of a diary is a nice personal touch, as is a map of the town; also a list of agency facilities and resources if these are available, so that the student does not have to enquire about them all the time. Lastly, the whereabouts of the tea- and coffee-making facilities and the toilets are important. As much information as possible should be put into writing, as it is difficult to remember detail, especially under the pressures of a new experience, and it can save a student making constant time-consuming reference to other people.

Planning the student's first week

This is the period of role induction proper of the student into his or her role as a learner/practitioner in the agency. Taken to their extreme, there are probably two basic models of inducting a student into the placement:

1. *The planned programme approach*, in which most of the time is taken up by a series of sessions throughout the week. This can be referred to as the deductive or taught approach to induction.

2. *The acquire-it-as-you-go-along approach*. This can be described as the inductive approach, where the student picks up the information in a more informal way via 'natural' exposure to the agency.

With the *planned programme approach*, the emphasis of the first week is on imparting to the student knowledge about the agency, its resources and its relationships with other agencies. The more informal, *inductive approach* emphasises the requirement on the part of students to take opportunities to

acquire this knowledge as they assume their new role in placements. Whether a supervisor takes one or other of these approaches in their extreme form depends on:
1. the inclinations of the student;
2. the exigencies of the placement, e.g. whether it is comparatively short;
3. the efficiency of the student in getting into the role quickly;
4. the needs of the agency in protecting the interests of its clients and the smoothness of its organisation.

It is probably a question of finding a balance between these two extremes, through taking into account the above factors. We will describe the likely content of each of these approaches.

The planned programme approach

This planned induction programme may be the only opportunity in an entire career that students have to explore systematically the administration and resources of the agency in which they are placed, and those of other agencies with which it frequently collaborates. Seen in that light it can be a golden opportunity to lay down the foundations of a knowledgeable future practice. On the other hand, there is the danger of overwhelming students, so that they become either exhausted by the process or bored with assimilating information which may seem to have little relevance to their immediate work concerns. Useful principles to bear in mind in planning an induction programme for a student are:
(a) finding a balance between the student's ability to take in new information and to digest it; and
(b) the dangers of over-learning and of a severe falling-off on the learning curve, which makes some sessions unproductive and even counterproductive.

The informal inductive approach

In using this approach emphasis is given to introducing students promptly to the work they will undertake in the placement. It reflects a belief that students are more likely to be motivated to acquire knowledge of the resources of the agency and other agencies when they need it for use, and that they will learn a great deal about those resources in the course of their work.

If, as the placement progresses, the practice teacher is to avoid being mis-used as the only source of knowledge, the student will need to be encouraged to take opportunities to visit relevant sections of the placement agency and other agencies. Otherwise there is a danger that the student will simply acquire a superficial and fragmented knowledge of resources, which may lead to partial, ill-informed actions in their work with clients. It is helpful to encourage the student to consult other sources of information, such as leaflets, books and agency reports.

Examples of the models

The following examples are taken from supervisors' reports, which describe their perspective on the approach they have taken and give illustrations of learning opportunities they have arranged for their students.

Example 1: an example of a planned programme approach from an interim assessment report of a student in her main placement in a social services department area team.

> To enable Jennifer to familiarise herself with the area at the agency, the first three weeks of the placement were devoted to a pre-arranged induction programme. She spent this time observing, visiting and meeting the various people and resources that social workers are in regular contact with, e.g. welfare rights, staff in various homes, area specialist staff, etc. Jennifer also participated in weekly team and allocation meetings and observed other social workers on the duty desk. This time was specifically set aside to provide Jennifer with a working knowledge of the agency, but she has obviously continued to learn and to develop her knowledge throughout the placement.

Example 2: Another example of a planned programme approach is provided by a student intending to enter the probation service, in her first placement, in a social services area team.

The first two weeks were spent as a general introduction. She spent time in discussion with each team member in which they outlined their general work. Sandra attended an allocation meeting of the intake team, spent one day with a home help organiser and one with the occupational therapist, followed by half a day each with a street warden organiser, a child minder (the volunteer organiser's post was vacant), and a social worker for the blind. She was also allowed access through the training senior to the area library. In an effort to give her further experience relevant to the sort of cases she would like to have, she spent half a day in court with our court officer and a day working at an old people's home. Subsequently . . . she spent half a day at two different day nurseries, a day with a health visitor, a day at a day centre for the physically handicapped, half a day at our welfare rights office, and an afternoon at a children's home.

The following are examples of the inductive, informal approach to a student's induction into the work of an agency.

Example 3: this illustration concerns a student in her main placement in a social services area team.

in the course of her work Lucy has visited homes for the elderly and a day centre for recovering mentally ill. She has liaised over cases with GPs, home help organisers and voluntary organis-ations. Lucy has accompanied myself as an observer on visits and has 'sat in' to assist on office duty days.

Example 4: this example concerns a third and final placement student in a social services area team.

Heather needed very few observational visits – mainly because of her very positive manner of introducing herself to situations with legitimate reasons for visiting or asking for information. She is very good at extracting the maximum amount of interest and value to her work out of the most minimal contacts with people and places.

Example 5: this illustration concerns a student Laura who is in her main placement with a voluntary agency specialising in the adoption and fostering of difficult-to-place children.

She has undertaken joint visits to families and children's homes with social workers from the project, in order to gain an overall picture of the types of children that we are working with. From the beginning of the placement Laura has used all project staff to extend her knowledge . . . throughout the placement Laura has been willing to gain extra knowledge and has made good use of the project's library. In the case of Denise she has found it relevant to look at the problems associated with adult schizophrenics and visited a local psychiatric hospital and discussed the problems with the social worker.

Whatever decision the practice teacher makes in the form of the induction programme, its content in the first week or two will address the following aspects:
1. an introduction to the work of the agency and its staff;
2. an introduction to resources and other relevant agencies;
3. an introduction to the student's personal work.
We will now look at those three aspects in turn.

The agency and its staff

The act of introducing students to their immediate colleagues in the team is not a superficial courtesy, but a final act of planning, which began much earlier in the stage of preplacement planning. For a student placement to be effective requires that the members of the immediate team fully accept the student on placement. They must perceive him/her as a social worker in training, entitled to full membership of the team (a good empirical test of this is whether the student will be able to attend team meetings) and fully involved in the earlier contract-making stage in the planning. The practice teacher should have worked through with colleagues any ambivalence about having a student. There must be a real acceptance that taking a student demands additional time and energy, breaks up established rhythms and routines in the group, and may take interesting work away from some colleagues. A student may also take up some of their time directly. Introductions, then, should be a symbolic act confirming the real acceptance of the student, reflecting an active involvement of the team in the decision to take the student.

Occasionally a team may be going through a difficult period in its relationships at the time the student begins the placement. How should the supervisor handle this? As a student is going to be a part of the team, and as long as the difficulties are general knowledge in the team, then it seems appropriate to ensure that the student is made aware of them. The student is going to meet the conflicts anyway. The difficulties should be explained to the student in terms of the history and development of the team, but emphasis should be given to the way the conflicts influence the team's functioning. If the conflicts involve the supervisor personally, then it may be difficult to be impartial, and perhaps explanations should be left to the team leader. Aside from these difficulties, a supervisor could ask colleagues to give brief pen portraits of themselves, in writing, for the student, in the same way as they have been provided with one of the student.

There will usually be other people, beyond team colleagues to introduce during the first few days. A balance should be maintained between sheer numbers, tact and courtesy, and the need for the student to function effectively through co-operative relationships with other people. Introductions can serve a number of purposes. They can be symbolic, for example the introduction to the person in charge of the agency (although it should be recognised that it is in the nature of bureaucracies that staff must learn to work without much direct contact with senior managers; nonetheless, senior staff are often interested in keeping in touch with the new generations of students, however impressionistically). There are also introductions which are functional for good work, which we mentioned earlier. Then there are those people who may be contributing in a more formal way to the students's induction programme. Finally, there are introductions which are largely a matter of courtesy, to people with whom the student is unlikely to have direct contact, except in special cases.

Introduction to the resources of the agency and other key agencies

The guiding factors here are the agency's need for efficient performance by the student, the work that a student is likely to undertake, and his or her ability to digest numerous and varied pieces of information. The following are considerations:

1. Students may have to absorb information in a more methodical way because of the artificial length of the placement.
2. They may never again have such an opportunity to acquaint themselves with the resources and functions of the agency.
3. They are also on placement not only to learn how to do the agency's work, but to learn how the agency functions.

With respect to introductions to representatives of other agencies, the supervisor will take into account both the demands of the placement for the student and the functioning of the agency generally. It will be important to brief the contributors beforehand, both on what the supervisor wants them to cover and how to cover it. Hopefully, the talks should complement the reading the student should have undertaken for the placement. Although contributors should cover all the main functions of their agency, they should do it using a broad brush-stroke, so that the student can compare the account with his/her own reading, without being lost in detail. In addition the student will want to know how that particular agency compares and differs with similar agencies in other areas.

An introduction to the personal workload

This should take place early on in the induction phase, because it is the main motivating force for the student in coming to the placement. The student is a personal service worker and not an administrator. How this is done and what work is assigned at this stage depends on the tasks to be undertaken, whether the student has done similar work before, and the student's knowledge of the agency. If a student has not undertaken actual practice before, then it may be helpful for him or her to sit in on colleagues' interviews and to observe on visits to a client's home. This can provide a useful perspective for the student from which to view his/her own performance, without the implication of needing to imitate.

An issue that is sometimes raised by practice teachers at this stage is whether students should be permitted, or indeed be required, to read existing files on the clients, or encouraged to form their own impressions from direct contact only. Students, and indeed new workers, often have strong views on this issue. Our own view is that we would normally require the student to read the file first, certainly before beginning systematic work with a client. There is an obligation to the client, who may well be relying on the continuity of work with a previous social worker. To do otherwise seems to imply a devaluation of the previous approach with a client, without any basis for it. In our view an approach to work should be related to the problem hypothesis, or proven method, rather than the inclination of the practitioner, unless the previous method is demonstrably ineffective. In the latter case there is a sound argument for the existing approach to give way to a theoretically more valid, but unproven approach, or indeed one that is both proven and to which the student inclines. To the objection that a student may be unduly influenced by the previous approach of a worker and thus prevented from making up his/her own mind about the case, we would say that they ought to be influenced. A student who cannot use information discriminately is going to have great difficulty as a learner, and may as well be helped to overcome the problem at this early stage as later.

Some tasks assigned to a student may be transferred from the existing work of other colleagues. It is probably not a good idea in general to transfer long-standing cases for the duration of a placement, and there are those mythical cases which are allegedly passed on from student to student. However, there may be a case or a task which is to be transferred to the student where the worker is leaving the agency and where the work is likely to be completed during the placement, as well as those more common transfers of cases created by intake teams in social services departments or probation agencies. The practice teacher should remember that a transferred case is a terminated case, and the student should be prepared to work through any unresolved issues which arise from ending the previous relationship, and which may complicate the forming of the new one.

New work, whether cases to be assigned or tasks, raises the issue of how the student is to be designated within the agency, to outside agencies, and to clients. We think it is useful to think of students as social workers in training, and indeed some of them have undertaken the role of unqualified social workers before coming to their courses. In referring to them as students there is a danger of the client becoming concerned about the student's competence. Unless the agency is going to give clients a choice as to whether they have someone in training to help them with their problems, it seems more straightforward to refer to the student by the well understood role designation of 'social worker'. A similar approach should be adopted with other agencies with whom there will be a continuing relationship, unless there are letters which go out formally in the name of the head of the agency. Within the agency it is important to make clear that the student is in a protected learning role, and not a full-time member of the agency.

As far as the assignment of new work is concerned, it should be borne in mind that teaching and learning starts on the first day of the placement. To assign cases or tasks at an early stage is to invoke the inductive model rather than the planned programme approach. The student can be asked to read the case papers or background papers and to prepare thoughts on how to begin the work on the case. For the supervisor, it is a case of starting as you intend to go on.

The student should be invited to consider the implications for intervention on the basis of the information available. There should then be a consultation to discuss the student's views. A test of whether the student has a reasonable grasp of the possible eventualities in the case is whether the client is likely to suffer adversely from the consequences of the intervention. The student should then be allowed to begin the work of applying the intervention. This process usefully applies to cases, or to the beginning stages of a project. The principle is to give the student from the beginning as much responsibility for the case as is commensurate with the proper handling of the tasks involved.

To reiterate, then, the general principles for allocating work tasks to the student are as follows:
1. account should be taken of the student's stage of professional development;
2. the student should in all liklihood be successful in dealing with the initial tasks allocated;
3. the work should not create aversive reactions in the student early on.

The features of a manageable case or task are as follows:
1. the clients to be helped should be motivated and co-operative, even if ambivalent;
2. there should be a clearly defined problem or need;
3. there should not be too many subsidiary problems;
4. the feelings associated with the work should not be strongly negative.

The supervisor's preparations revisited

We have outlined the considerations which a supervisor should have in mind in the immediate preparations for the student's arrival. There may be further considerations, of a more general kind, which they can bring to bear.

The period of setting the scene for learning is a final opportunity to decide on a preferred style of supervision for the placement. The expectations that are set at this point may be difficult to break out of at a later stage in the placement. We suggest that it is best to see the practice teacher role as a facilitator of the student's learning, which on occasion involves teaching the student directly. It can be balanced with a more indirect role, emphasising that the student's work experience itself may be the best form of instruction, with other people teaching the student and the student involved in self-teaching and learning.

The student has come to learn and not simply to work. The supervisor's job is to ensure that the student is not only learning, but learning the correct things. Unhelpful learning can take place as well as positive learning. The supervisor may not be required to teach everything, but simply to be the person with authority to check that:

(a) learning is taking place
(b) correct learning is taking place
(c) sufficient learning is taking place.
It is the supervisor's task to ensure that the student is not being asked to take in more than he can learn without stress, i.e. what Towle (1954) calls the 'integrative task exceeding the integrative capacity'. Similarly, the supervisor should not allow a situation to be created where more performing, and thus learning, is taking place than the supervisor can evaluate and discuss with the student. There is a need to find a balance between:
(a) the amount of work the student does
(b) the amount of study of various kinds related to that work
(c) the supervisor getting access to that understanding, and
(d) evaluating the quality of the learning that is taking place.

The idea of the placement: student and supervision

Many modern social work agencies are very large and meet increasingly diverse needs. They require a greater degree of specialisation on the part of staff, and increasingly staff are not experts over a great range of work or in any great detail. The size of the administration requires an increasingly bureaucratic organisation, and a student has to learn to work through delegated authority. This involves learning to work with and through other people, and it may be as important to learn how to release the helping power of the agency as to engage in direct work with clients.

The student may well come to the placement with already acquired methods of intervention with which the supervisor is unfamiliar. A student will nonetheless be entitled to try them out, as long as they are equally valid and responsible methods to those customarily used in the agency. It may be appropriate for the supervisors to limit their role to an evaluation of the validity of the method to the particular case or task at hand. It will be up to the student to demonstrate the competence and validity of the innovation, and perhaps the tutor can interpret and facilitate the link between the traditional and the new.

Increasingly, supervisors may not be able to give direct teaching in every area of the student's work and it will be appropriate to 'farm out' some of the aspects of the work to other colleagues. Nonetheless, they will retain the responsibility to protect the notion of the generic learning of the student in preparation for the role of social worker and to evaluate and assess the overall performance of the student. This leads us to the supervisory relationship itself.

5

The Supervision Session

During practice placements, the social work student is subject to a continuous process of informal learning: by participating in office discussions, by observing colleagues' attitudes, and by overhearing their telephone conversations. Supervision sessions, however, provide the formal context for teaching and learning and demand more of the supervisor than simply being available to discuss the next step on a piece of work. This chapter looks at the nature and purpose of supervision. We suggest ways of planning and structuring the supervision session, introducing a range of ideas about the principles and the process skills that the supervisor needs.

The nature of supervision

It is important to define what we mean by supervision and to differentiate between supervision and what is sometimes referred to as supervision, but is in fact consultation. By *supervision*, we mean planned, regular periods of time that student and supervisor spend together discussing the student's work in the placement and reviewing the learning progress. While negotiating the placement, student and supervisor will have discussed their expectations with regard to supervision: its frequency, duration, the content of supervision sessions, and the priority it should be accorded. Because of the pressures of other work, it can happen that supervisors do not always treat supervision as a priority which should only be altered if absolutely necessary. We are by no means suggesting that the supervision sessions should be the only opportunity for student and supervisor to discuss the student's work. Frequently, in order that the student can move on to the next stage in a piece of work, he or she will also need on-the-spot *consultation*, which need not necessarily be from the supervisor. The student might consult with a team colleague, or with the senior or a specialist worker, such as a fostering officer or court officer.

> The consultant does not carry administrative accountability and therefore is not responsible for the implementation of the recommended action. The professional responsibility remains with the consultee . . . who is free to accept or reject the advice and make of it what she will (Westheimer, 1977).

Thus the student might consult elsewhere for advice, but the accountability for any subsequent decision lies with the supervisor. However experienced a student might be, consultation is not a substitute for supervision.

The main purpose of the practice placement is to provide students with opportunities to become involved in helping clients – to test themselves out in the role of social worker. The primary task for supervisors is to maximise the opportunities for students to learn for themselves, within the context of the particular agency setting. The supervisor, therefore, has two roles to perform: that of supervisor and that of practice teacher. The supervisor is accountable to both the agency and the client; the practice teacher has a responsibility to the educational establishment and the student. The supervisor has, first, to ensure that a good standard of service is offered to the agency's clients, and, second, to develop skills in teaching so as to maximise the learning for the student.

Priscilla Young (1967) sees the supervisor as part of the teaching team, as an educator, whose duties include:

(a) Planning and producing a programme of learning opportunities which is a recognisable entity, not a series of disconnected experiences.

(b) Providing help in learning for students, through enabling them to understand the meaning of their experience of helping clients, as well as through the direct giving of information.

(c) Creating a climate for learning, which includes as its

main focus their relationship, through which the student will get encouragement and feedback and help in integrating theoretical knowledge with practical experience.

(d) Helping the student with personal feelings of a more stressful kind, which may be aroused through the process of involvement in the work.

Allocation of work to the student

Planning appropriate work for students should reflect the agreed learning tasks of any placement. The work students undertake provides the focus for learning and needs to be appropriate to their level of ability. In order, therefore, that students are neither insufficiently stretched, nor overwhelmed by trying to deal with complex tasks which they do not yet have the skills to manage, the allocation of work is crucially important and should be carefully controlled by the supervisor. This should ensure that the 'games' which can be set up at allocation meetings are avoided: for example, the old cry of 'this sounds an ideal case for a student!' (Gallop and Quinn, 1981), resulting in unfair pressure on the student to accept the case; or the situation where a student indiscriminately takes on any work on offer, much to the relief of team colleagues. Two other situations to avoid are:

1. The temptation continually to cream off the more interesting work to the student, thereby possibly antagonising colleagues; or
2. allowing the student to be allocated work which nobody else is prepared to take on.

A useful general guide to the work that should be allocated is Pettes's dictum, that 'in whatsoever areas the student is to be evaluated, he must be taught' (Pettes, 1967). This means that before taking a student the supervisor needs to be aware of and to agree to the areas of evaluation that the particular education establishment has requested, so as to ensure that the student is allocated work in those areas. Some of the skills evaluated are more general ones arising out of the process of the work, for example, relationships with other agencies and relationships with colleagues. Other problems, needs and clients of the particular agency will dictate that more specific areas of knowledge and skills need to be evaluated.

The following criteria will guide a supervisor in the kind of work that might be allocated to the student:

1. The extent of the student's previous knowledge of the agency's work, or particular aspects of it.
2. The supervisor's view of a representative section of the agency's work which the student should undertake in order to justify the placement.
3. The confidence that the student brings to the placement; the areas of work he or she feels confident to explore and those about which they feel least confident.
4. The student's own expressed areas of interest.
5. The initial work should be, as far as it is possible to judge, within the competence of the student, so that the work is likely to be successfully completed.
6. The amount of work offered to the student at any time should be within his or her capacity, with some balance between quality and quantity.
7. The amount of work undertaken should be within the capacity of the supervisor to study, so that carefully considered evaluation of the student's performance is feasible.

Initial allocation of work provides supervisors with their first opportunity to assess the way the student approaches the work. It is also the first opportunity for supervisors to practise restraint in their own role towards the student. The less involved supervisors are, the more likely they are to perceive and learn how the student initiates work on a given task.

It has been suggested that students characteristically respond to new work in one of two ways:

1. The first is to explore, analyse and understand the possible parameters of the presenting problem before taking action. This student is more likely to want to discuss aspects of the case with the supervisor at the point of allocation.
2. The second is to initiate action on the information available, discovering what is involved in the situation through involvement in it. This student will want to discuss what happened with the supervisor afterwards.

In their more extreme forms, these students might be identified as those who can 'think but not act' and those who can 'act but not reflect'. The supervisor's task will be to assess how the student's approach to the work affects the service provided to clients.

It may be that the student's preferred learning style is inappropriate in certain circumstances. A social worker cannot always know everything before taking action, and in many situations the first task is to gather information, whether it be from the individual client or from members of the community. On the other hand, a student also needs to be encouraged to gather whatever information is available, for example from a dormant file, before rushing out to undertake work that may duplicate earlier failed interventions.

Planning for supervision

The following are aspects of supervision that we suggest need to be considered in planning the overall supervision of a student.

The student will want to know that there is a planned, regular time when the supervisor will be available to them. Apart from anything else, this will help the student to plan his or her work, as it will act indirectly as a deadline within which to complete tasks. Frequency and timing of supervision sessions can be negotiated, usually when the contract is made between the student and supervisor. It is useful to have a time – limited session so that the student and supervisor know what is expected. Where a student, for example, shows a tendency to want to discuss a case immediately after visiting (or indeed if the need is expressed by the supervisor) care must be taken to question whether this is justified or whether the student should be discouraged from this practice. It is an easy habit for both to fall into and can impede a student's development and sense of responsibility for his/her own work. For this reason it is important for the student to know exactly when there will be the opportunity for discussion.

Expectations about the student's preparation for supervision should be made clear. As the work done by the student is the focus for learning, students are required to share their experience with their supervisor, so that the work is open to be supervised. This provides the supervisor with the opportunity to confirm good work, to identify and reinforce learning, to draw attention to areas that have been missed, and to the consequences of issues that have not been handled well. There is a number of ways in which students share their work:

1. through written records of their work;
2. through discussion with their supervisor;
3. through the use of special methods of recording, for example the process record, direct observation by the supervisor, tape recording and video recording.

Students need to know what they are required to produce for the supervision session, so that the necessary preparation can be done.

The above methods of producing evidence of work for the purpose of evaluation are considered in more detail in Chapters 6 and 7. By far the most common method used is discussion. We suggest that in planning supervision sessions, consideration is given to using a variety of methods because (a) the style of supervision can get 'fixed', and using a variety of methods can make the process more interesting; (b) the supervisor will be encouraging the student to use a variety of methods of intervention and will therefore be able to offer a model through the variety of methods used in supervision; and (c) different methods will give the supervisor access to different aspects of the quality of the student's performance and thus of his or her learning.

We have mentioned the student's preparation for supervision sessons. It is important, too, for the supervisor to prepare – to study recordings and reports produced, as the student will be expecting feedback.

Not only can the style of supervision become stale, but the conduct of supervision sessions can be repetitive. Too often supervision is focused entirely on the student's activities. Student and supervisor could agree to commit themselves to studying a particular piece of relevant legislation, for example, or a review of the services to a particular client group, or a method of working, in preparation for discussion at the next supervision session.

A further consideration for supervisors is to make provision for students to obtain advice when they are not available themselves. Who should students approach to discuss their work if their supervisor is off sick, on holiday or simply not available when the students feel they urgently need to discuss a problem? In most situations this will usually be a senior colleague, but in some voluntary agencies there might be no other member of staff, or no person other than the supervisor in a senior position. Not knowing a named person to approach can cause unnecessary worry for students.

It can be useful not only to plan the duration of the supervision sessions, but also to plan a rough agenda at the beginning of the session. Both supervisor and student will probably have areas they wish to discuss; by noting these at the beginning of the session, all items are likely to be dealt with, or at worst postponed but noted for a subsequent session. Open-ended, unplanned supervision sessions can tend to ramble indiscriminately, with the students feeling frustrated, because what was urgent to them, but perhaps not to their supervisors, is not given adequate time. Clearly it is the responsibility of supervisors not to let this happen.

The opposite concern to the one above is the danger of over-structuring the supervision session and thereby, for example, inhibiting discussion. Anxious supervisors, lacking confidence in their ability to stimulate an academically bright student, may feel so threatened that they are tempted to over-control and limit discussions to the parameters within which they feel comfortable.

Finally, a reminder about the 'contract'. We have suggested earlier that this is the cornerstone of the placement and have suggested that adequate time and consideration should be given to preparing it. Having produced a clear contract, it is important to use it in a placement to ascertain whether learning goals have been achieved and whether the placement is 'on target'.

The process of supervision

The function of supervision is to help the student become aware of the nature of the job to be learned and to acquire the knowledge and skills involved in responding to people's needs in a helpful way.

In the supervision session, the supervisor should be aware that there are two things to deal with at the same time:

1. the educational process, i.e. helping the student to identify and to make explicit learning already acquired, by asking questions such as: 'What led you to this conclusion?'; 'What knowledge are you using when you make that assumption?'; 'What concepts are you using?'
2. the social work content: the knowledge and skills that are relevant to the problem in hand.

The process of supervision in relation to any issue can be seen to follow a number of stages, which we have identified below, and which contain their own particular tasks, skills and techniques.

The descriptive stage

Initially the supervisor has to listen to and attempt to understand the problem or situation as seen by the student, whether this is in relation to a case or any other project. It is important that students be allowed to convey their understanding of the situation first, because this will enable them to remain in control of the work, and to feel a sense of responsibility for it. Students should therefore be given an open-ended invitation to have their say, with the minimum intrusion by the supervisor, so as not to break the flow of their communication.

During this stage a supervisor will need to encourage the student, withholding criticism but avoiding reinforcement of any poor practice. Although it may be necessary to ask for information in order to resolve pertinent questions in the supervisor's own mind and to structure the discussion where necessary, the supervisor should try to avoid thoughtless questions, which may merely confuse the student. A good test of the validity of a question during this stage is to envisage the response that would be made if the student asked the supervisor what they were getting at in asking the question. It is often useful to volunteer what the point of a question is, and this should especially be done where the student appears puzzled or uncertain about the reason for it.

It is very important at this stage to ensure that the case is left firmly with the student and to avoid what we call 'we-ism'. There can be a tendency for supervisors to talk about a piece of work as if it is theirs as well as the student's; as if the case is being jointly worked. Clearly there is a sense in which the supervisor has a responsibility for the case or project which the student is handling, but we would suggest that it does not amount to a joint responsibility for the work, otherwise students never aquire a sense of responsibility for their own skills in exercising discretion, taking initiatives and choosing the approach that is to be used.

The stage of clarification

The aim in this stage is to establish with the student that the supervisor has understood the situation as it is seen by the student and understands the work the student has been doing. There are usually two related issues at stake in any supervision discussion: the student both brings an objective problem for discussion, i.e. one which is primarily to do with the work itself and can be understood independently of the student; and the second, and the most important as far as the student's learning is concerned, is the problem as the student has perceived it, including the reason why they have brought it to supervision. The two problems may not be synonymous, as the student may be having certain difficulties with the case which are not simply to do with the objective problems contained within it. It is important to ensure that the proper focus is on the student's problem with the case, if he or she is to continue to feel responsible for it and in control of their work. Students' problems will sometimes be to do with the feelings they have in relation to the situation.

The evaluative stage

Students will be seeking confirmation of the way they have handled the case or task and, at this point, the supervisor will need to go back over the work, affirming the positive parts, ensuring that the student knows why these are good, and identifying those aspects which seem to be a problem.

The general principle at this stage of discussion is to draw out of the student (a) the student's understanding of the problem, and (b) that part of the student's knowledge that is relevant to the situation.

In this stage it will also be necessary to help the student identify the learning issues in the situation. This may be in terms of increasing understanding of the problem, acquiring information as to relevant resources available, or increasing skills in particular methods of working. It may be necessary to do some direct teaching at this point or to suggest that the student should undertake some research into resources available, or for the supervisor to explain a certain procedure.

The implementation stage

The aim of this final stage is to enable the student to progress with the case: to take the next step. Again, it is important to ascertain first where the student thinks he or she can go with the case and why. If the approach is appropriate, the supervisor will need to confirm it. If the student is stuck, encouragement will be needed to consider different possibilities. This is the time to introduce relevant knowledge, offering suggestions as to alternative ways of understanding or of intervening. The golden rule at this stage is not to go far beyond the student's present stage of learning. If the supervisor 'loses' the student, the latter will feel demoralised. There is a danger that the supervisor will go on an 'ego trip', displaying their own knowledge, which might be far in advance of the student's, and introduce too many new ideas too quickly. It is also important to remember that a supervisor is not responsible for the pace at which the student is able to learn. The supervisor must try to facilitate students' learning and to avoid holding them up.

Finally, both student and supervisor need to be satisfied that as much work as possible in the time available has been done on the material/topic for supervision. The student should feel able to move on confidently, and the supervisor should ensure that any areas of concern have been discussed and resolved.

The focus of supervision

In examining any piece of work with the student, the supervisor is likely to be focusing on one or more of the following areas:

1. The student's capacity to understand the nature of the basic problem. Without this understanding, the student will not be able to plan a strategy for intervention or act in a more than immediate helping capacity.

2. The student's ability to handle the problems presented at the different stages of the work. For example, in casework problems might arise in forming a relationship, negotiating a contract, assessment, planning treatment, or in termination and evaluation. Each of these stages in the helping process provides opportunities for helping to resolve the client's particular problems.

3. The knowledge requirements of particular cases, which may only be partially known or understood by the student. These may be to do with legislation, statutory requirements, administrative procedures, theoretical inputs, empirical experience, – for example, the effects of separation on children and parents – the resources available; and alternative techniques.

4. The capacity to form and maintain appropriate relationships, that is, the relationships necessary to enable the particular task to be carried out to a conclusion which is as successful as possible.

5. The capacity to formulate goals, plan strategies of action and initiate and carry them out.

6. Personal reactions to the problems presented, particularly those creating worry and anxiety. All learning entails a certain amount of worry, due to the gap between students' understanding and their ability to resolve a problem. But some problems may be too severe for the student to cope with, or it may be that it presents a particular threat. Examples are aggression, death, sexuality, chaos, rejection.

7. Indications that the student is expressing professional values in the work or is aware of threats to them from other people; for example, a client's right to determine their own life.

Feedback

One of the main responsibilities of the supervisor in the supervision session is to give feedback to the student. Feedback is the process of relaying to a person observations, impressions, feelings or other evaluative information about that person's behaviour for their own use and learning. Receiving feedback is essential to the student's progress. Without it students have no way of thoroughly evaluating their work; self-evaluation is insufficient. Providing effective feedback therefore enables an individual to modify ineffective behaviour and serves to reinforce effective work.

Effective feedback should be helpful to the person receiving it. It must be given in such a way that the receiver (a) understands clearly what is being communicated, and (b) is able to accept the information.

Guidelines for giving effective feedback

1. It should be requested by the receiver.
2. It should be given as promptly as possible.
3. It should be given in non-technical language.
4. It should be concise: that is, it must not contain more detail than was present in the work on which feedback is being given.
5. It should focus on the individual's specific and observable behaviour as opposed to their character. For example, it is better to say, 'you don't look at me when you talk to me', than 'you are strange or distant'.
6. It should be given in a personal, helpful, non-threatening manner and should avoid value or moral judgements. For example, say 'when you don't look at me when I'm talking, I feel you are not listening', rather than 'no-one likes people who refuse to have eye contact'.
7. It should concentrate only on behaviour over which the individual has some control.
8. It should focus on the individual's strengths as well as weaknesses.
9. It should be discussed by the giver and the receiver until they can agree on what is being communicated.

The supervisory relationship

Any learning requires change, and change invariably creates anxiety. The supervisory relationship generates a number of anxieties for students: there is the threat to their independence and autonomy; the anxiety of exposing their ignorance and vulnerability; the risk of not meeting their supervisor's expectations. The threat of change is greater for the adult in training: it often demands radical changes in attitudes and patterns of thinking that have become fixed over the years. It requires identification with new models and the subsequent rejection of previously held ideas. However confident students may appear, or however impressive their previous experience, the supervisor needs to be aware of the context in which the learning takes place and to be prepared to handle issues sensitively.

The relationship is also threatening to the supervisor. In the nature of their role supervisors have a desire to be seen as helpful, and for their contributions to be considered informative and relevant. However, there may be anxiety that the student will expose their limitations, that their attitudes and methods will be challenged, or that the student will reject them. In an attempt to deal with their anxiety, supervisors may fall into the trap of becoming over-controlling, their control being exercised through over-use of their 'authority', 'previous training', or 'experience'.

In chapter 2, we suggested that aspiring supervisors need to make an honest appraisal of their own strengths and weaknesses. For supervision to achieve maximum effectiveness, the supervisory relationships needs to be based on maximum participation by both supervisor and student. Although the supervisor is in the more powerful position in the relationships, this is not to suggest that learning is a one-way affair, with the supervisor always in the teaching role. As Westheimer (1977) says, 'the supervisor must herself believe in ongoing learning and progress', and that if the supervisor 'does not enjoy learning herself she is unlikely to make a good supervisor'.

Mutual participation in the learning process demands a wide variety of involvement by the supervisor, who must be willing to risk the possibility of the student's hostility or rejection. Traditionally, social work supervision was seen as exerting pressure to conform to agency norms, and although a certain amount of socialisation to the social work role takes place through the process of supervision, the supervisor needs to allow the student to challenge the policies of the agency and the supervisor's approach to practice.

What is needed is an honest sharing of feelings and attitudes, knowledge and information which will enable the student to learn in the most unthreatened way. Supervisors who are able to recognise and acknowledge both their strengths and weaknesses, who are able to say 'I don't know', are less vulnerable to being engaged in 'gamesmanship' – strategies which may allay anxieties at the expense of the student's development.

Games people play in supervision

Eric Berne, in *Games People Play* (Berne, 1964), defines a game as 'an ongoing series of complementary ulterior trans-actions – superficially plausible, but with a concealed motivation'. We think it worthwhile giving examples of the more common strategies that supervisors and students can find themselves employing when difficulties arise in the super-visory relationship.

Example A: the supervisor wants to be seen as helpful and offers to be available and supportive all the time. This arises when supervisors lack confidence in their role. Their insecurity might stem from anxiety about whether they have enough to offer; whether they will meet the student's or the educational establishment's expectations. The resulting strategy might be for supervisors to over-identify with students, colluding with them against the agency or educational establishment. This may result, for example, in administrative functions being neglected, or given low priority, or dismissed as being unnecessary bureaucratic evils. The danger here is that a supervisor becomes hesitant to exert authority, thus avoiding 'making firm decisions or giving instructions which are necessary for the protection of clients' (Westheimer, 1977). Some supervisors choose to deny the element of authority in the supervisory relationship, perhaps fearing rejection. The game employed here is one of emotional blackmail: 'I'm being nice to you and I expect you to be considerate to me'. The consequence is a cosy relationship in which little learning takes place.

Example B: the strategy employed by a supervisor who controls areas of discussion and ideas. It arises out of poor matching of student and supervisor. For example, a student who is described as 'good academically and a voracious reader' is placed with a supervisor who has never been a great reader and has done little 'technical' reading since qualifying several years ago. The supervisor may plan supervision sessions well ahead, thereby not always coinciding with the student's learning needs. This practice teacher might have difficulty relating theory to practice in a constructive way and could be unhelpful to a student who needs a lot of teaching input and encouragement in conceptualising theories and models and how to apply them. A resultant ploy by the student might be to make the running: 'I'd like to know more about family therapy', or, 'Have you read the new book on . . .'. The supervisor might set up the student in the intellectual role, deferring to the student; supervision sessions might then be spent on the student supplying knowledge. Alternatively the supervisor might denigrate intellectual thinking, and refuse to engage in positive and meaningful discussions because it is 'irrelevant' or 'too philosophical'. There may be a deliberate attempt to avoid issues that may lead to innovation or the educational and personal development of the student.

Example C: this arises when a student initiates the game: 'If you give me work, I'll be uncritical and you won't have any problems with me'. These students, reluctant to be pushed intellectually, always want new work, new situations, volunteering for work at allocation meetings, then excusing themselves as being too busy. The supervisor, anxious about the standard of the student's work and the effect on the client, becomes more controlling, limits the amount of work, and begins to interfere in cases, thus taking away responsibility for the work from the student. One of the most difficult aspects of the transition from practitioner to supervisor is allowing students to take responsibility for their own work; the tendency is to want to take over, particularly if there is some difficulty. Unfortunately, as Westheimer says, 'the supervisor cannot do the worker's learning for him and has to allow him to experiment to find his own way of dealing with a given situation'. The over-controlling supervisor reinforces dependency in a student; as the level of the supervisor's participation increases, so the student's involvement decreases. For supervisor's this is a difficult 'game' to avoid, as they are achieving considerable gratification from displaying their knowledge. The student can manipulate the situation by admitting ignorance: 'what would you do next?', 'how should I handle this?'. So the student invites reassurance and offloads responsibility! The final phase of this type of game is when the student turns to a supervisor and says: 'I did exactly what you told me and look how it turned out!'

6

Methods of Teaching and Learning (I)

The aim of this chapter and chapter 7 is to describe and analyse the strengths and weaknesses of a range of 'media' which are commonly and not so commonly used by supervisors in their teaching sessions with students. We believe that supervisors should not only use a number of methods for the sake of variety in their teaching sessions with students, but if they are to encourage their students to use a range of methods of interventions with their clients, then this ethos ought to be reflected in the supervisor's own work with students.

The following are a list of methods of supervision, or methods of teaching and learning, which one might expect to see being used in a placement: group supervision, co-working, didactic teaching, role play, audio and video taping, group supervision, client-based feedback, the discussion method, live supervision, process recording, rehearsal, case records, direct observation, written evaluations, case presentation, consultation and assigned reading. While the list of methods actually used is quite long, only a few of them would be used with any student in a single placement.

What the various methods have in common

What we have referred to in the title of this chapter as 'methods of teaching and learning' are commonly referred to by practice teachers as 'methods of supervision'. In reality they are methods through which teaching and learning take place, but they also serve a number of other important purposes:

1. To provide ways in which the student's performance is made accessible to the supervisor.
2. To enable learning to be confirmed (performance does not necessarily indicate that learning has taken place).
3. To enable further learning (general principles) to be established so that teaching can be offered by the supervisor.
4. To enable the quality of work and learning to be evaluated.

Learning

At this stage we would remind the reader of our earlier conception of learning as taking three forms:

1. Cognitive, or knowing and thinking, or analytical skills.
2. Affective, or feeling and valuing, or appropriate attitudes and values.
3. Behavioural, or acting and doing, or the carrying out of activities.

In performing work the student is required to bring together these three aspects of learning in a coherent way. Performance indicates that learning has taken place only if it also establishes that a student has understood the basis on which he or she has acted. Thus they have acted in a knowing way.

Methods of supervision are not in themselves secure evidence that learning has taken place. They are evidence of doing or performance, and a means of establishing the nature of a student's work. They are the only basis from which a supervisor can explore whether their student has made the proper connections between knowing, feeling and action, i.e. has undertaken their work with understanding.

A framework for understanding learning

It is probably useful to every supervisor to be able to combine a variety of methods of teaching and learning with a single, flexible framework or general model of learning, which they can use to analyse both the learning progress which their students are making and any problems they may be having. The strength of a variety of methods is that it (a) leads to a fairer basis for assessment, and (b) makes many more facets of a student's performance available for evaluation and teaching. References have been made earlier to a number of different models of learning, but at this stage we want to introduce an overall framework which can accommodate the other models and also be of very practical use for the supervisor. It is illustrated in Figure 6.1.

We are suggesting that every student's learning in a placement can be usefully conceptualised within the model; if problems arise, it will be possible to locate them in one or more of the stages of learning. For example, a student may be unable to proceed with a piece of work because of a lack of factual knowledge to begin to tackle the problem. On the other hand, the student may have the knowledge that is relevant to the problem, but may not be able to understand the implications of applying it to the issue at hand. Or it may be that a student has an intellectual understanding of how to apply knowledge to a particular problem, but their deficiency may lie in the ability to translate the understanding into action. The student may be too nervous, for example, to tackle a client who has a reputation for aggressiveness, or a client who is mentally unstable. Given that the student is able to overcome the problems of actually implementing the knowledge, he or she may then have difficulties in relating the consequences of the action to the original understanding. This will prevent the student from applying the understanding that derives from the intervention to subsequent interventions of a similar kind. The whole process then continues with a new cycle of understanding, application and analysis arising out of it and the possibilities of applying the new understanding to the next similar situation. A supervisor who finds that a student is stuck on a particular case or project ought to be able to find the source of the difficulty by locating it in one or more of those stages. The supervisor will then need a combination of educational principles and professional knowledge to help the student disentangle and resolve the problem, so that the

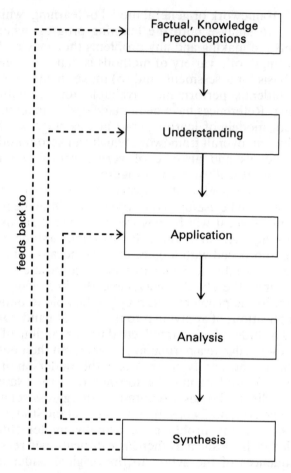

Figure 6.1 A simple flowchart to illustrate the learning cycle
Source: T. Hipgrave, Leicester University School of Social Work, 1984.

student can continue to make progress in his or her work and
learning.

Methods of supervision

It is our aim in the rest of this chapter to present a range of the
different methods of teaching and learning that are available

for use by the practice teacher. We will give a description of each, then examine the particular circumstances in which they may be used, their respective strengths and weaknesses as we see them, and the particular knowledge and skills that are needed to utilise them successfully.

The discussion method

This method is, of course, a component of all the other methods of supervision, as well as being a primary means by which learning is established as having taken place. We look on it as a method in itself when it is used as the sole means of exploring, evaluating and teaching about a piece of work.

Description. This method is being used when a student verbally relates to a supervisor what has been happening in the work. It is, of course, the most readily available method to a supervisor.

Advantages. One advantage is the amount of information that can be conveyed in the time available, as people talk more quickly than in any other form of communication. The supervisor also gains the immediacy of the feelings, thoughts and emotions that lie in the events being described. It is the least edited of the non-directly experienced reports of intervention. It has been argued that the process that takes place between student and client (or others) can also come through in the communication between the student and the supervisor, and thus a supervisor can experience it second hand. This has been described as the 'reflection' process in supervision (Mattinson, 1975).

Disadvantages. There may have been no opportunity for the student to reflect on his or her work beforehand, and to prepare learning points. The student has to think hurriedly and may miss points which he or she later decides were important. There is no record of the work or learning available, for further reflection, either by the student or the supervisor. In our view this is not a method on which supervisors should rely too heavily. However, it has a value when a student feels too anxious about a case to wait for a long period until the next supervision session, or where the session may be too close for them to write up the account beforehand. At the time it may be the only way the student feels can adequately convey his or her feelings about the work.

It is important that it does not become the only or main method of supervision. Supervisors always need ultimately to keep the boundary separate between what the student knows and what they themselves know, if learning is to be protected. With this method they can most easily become confused. They may also need to ensure that the record is written up by the student after a very emotional discussion, because there may be a reaction against the case by the student, which may make it difficult for them to face it.

Knowledge and skills. It is important to be attentive to the account, encouraging the flow of the events being described, listening carefully to the narrative and also to the tone of the account. Intervention should be limited to clarifying events until the problem is fully understood on the student's terms. The increasingly accomplished student will gradually be able to make a distinction between description, analysis and conclusion or synthesis, and this is an important skill to acquire. It will not, however, be expected of less experienced students, as it may be constraining, and some may need to be positively encouraged to let go so that more than a simple cognitive account is conveyed. Supervisors should be prepared to be themselves to the student, responding genuinely to the feelings and emotions that are conveyed and resisting the temptation to judge or to intervene with suggestions until the account is completed. The supervisor can then begin to use the model of learning described earlier in this chapter, which is appropriate to any of the methods being used.

Using work records

In using this method a supervisor is gaining access to the work through the written accounts submitted before the supervision session.

Circumstances. This is probably the best all-round method readily available and is probably the most common form of teaching and learning for a student. It provides a useful model for future work supervision, encourages work discipline, brings recording problems to the surface, and gets students to think for themselves and to declare their own learning positions first. In our view this is an important general method of indirect access to a student's work. In addition, we would suggest that a learning-oriented record is kept on some cases at least, separate from the agency record, especially where this may be required to be more succinct. A copy can be kept by both supervisor and student for the purpose of supervision.

Advantages. It provides an opportunity for the supervisor to reflect on the content of the work and to (a) prepare notes; (b) structure the points that will be raised; (c) refer to the previous record to see the pattern of the development of the work; (d) actually see how the student writes, e.g. spelling, grammar, style, etc., and (e) use it to teach about writing work records. A distinct advantage of the recording method, is that the supervisor obtains the student's view of the performance before it is clouded by later discussion.

Disadvantages. Like the discussion method, it is an indirect method of assessing the student's performance. The work being described may be dated, having been superseded by other events, and may need to be supplemented by the discussion method. The agency administrative records, particularly in hospitals, may not be adequately detailed for the purposes of teaching and learning. It may not be sufficiently clear what the student actually did, nor what the student learned from it.

Knowledge and skills. Supervisors tend to get what they deserve with this method. They should let the student know in advance what they expect from a written account:
1. A narrative account of the intervention.
2. An analysis of the student's own understanding of it.

3. The proposed next step in the work, based on the student's own analysis. Future actions should be based on understanding.

Any record should contain an adequate description of what has been undertaken, so that the supervisor can gain a reasonable picture of what the student actually did. Furthermore, the student should try to explain, or analyse, why he or she did particular things in the work. Where claims or assertions about the meaning of events are made, the student should be encouraged to support them with illustrations from the intervention or with evidence where substantial claims are being made. Finally, if possible, the student should begin to indicate the ways in which this understanding leads towards further possible courses of action.

The skills needed by the supervisor will depend on the quality of the record. If it is poorly written it may be that the student writes less well than he or she speaks. This can be checked through discussion. The student can then be asked to write a better record. If it is a good record, then the supervisor should resist treating it as if it is a discussion-based session. Instead the supervisor should:

1. Confirm the positive understandings and actions.
2. Clarify the meaning of obscure parts.
3. Draw out understandings which they believe may be there, but have not been recorded clearly.
4. Encourage the student to identify the important principles for generalisation and transfer to other work.

As always, the supervisor should encourage the student to take responsibility for what they know, understand and feel that they might act on.

Sitting in on a student's interview with a client or on indirect work for a client

By using this method the supervisor is gaining direct access to the student's ability to apply the knowledge, skills and techniques of practice in a particular situation. It may be done through a one-way screen, but in most situations it will involve sitting in the same room as the student, in a non-participative or perhaps semi-participative role. It should only be done with the prior agreement of the interviewee. Kingston and Smith (1983) and Ainley and Kingston (1981) have useful ideas to offer from their experience.

Cicumstances. We feel that this method should be a usual but minor part of the placement. It serves to confirm what the supervisor believes from other methods that the student is learning. It might be used to ensure fairness to a student about whose work there is concern from indirect methods of assessment. It can also be a more usual method of assessment where it is the policy of course tutors that a supervisor should offer direct evidence of a student's competence.

Advantages. The supervisor is gaining the most direct evidence of a student's performance in this aspect of practice, admittedly in what may be the worst circumstances for the student. If a student does all right in that situation, the supervisor can be confident that he or she can do at least as well in equivalent circumstances when they will not be present. The supervisor is being provided with a step-by-step account of the student's abilities. Being present in the situation allows the supervisor to get in touch with the subtler feelings of the interviewee and those of the student, which may be lost in video and audio recording. Ideally, the method serves to confirm positive impressions formed through other methods of supervision, or indeed to correct an erroneously poor view formed by other methods.

Disadvantages. It may put a lot of pressure on the student. It can also be time-consuming and is unlikely to be a regular source of information on the student's performance. It is often alleged to be off-putting to clients, although we know of no evidence for this, and many students and clients admit to forgetting about the observer after a few minutes. Other possible disadvantages are:
1. It may give a distorted picture because of the supervisor's presence, although this can be overstated.
2. It can be threatening to the student to introduce it as an idea if it was not included in the original contract for the placement.

3. The supervisor has to remember what went on in the interview and perhaps would be wise to take notes.
4. The supervisor may be expected to remember more accurately and objectively than the student.
5. There may be disagreement over what allegedly happened in the session, as well as on how it is to be construed.

Knowledge and skills. A supervisor needs to recognise that this method is threatening to the student and to make it clear whether or not it is being undertaken out of concern for the student's competence. Some over-anxious students may have fears that they will be 'seen through' as deficient for the first time. They should be de-briefed as soon as possible afterwards and time should be allowed for this. This (a) enables the supervisor to deal with any anxieties caused, and (b) avoids the danger of memories getting blurred after a time. Notes should be written immediately afterwards if discussion cannot take place straight away. Having established a basis for the discussion to follow, the supervisor should get the student to give his or her account of the interview, as with the discussion method.

Process recording

In this method students are required, after an interview, chairing a meeting, etc., to write it up in detail, giving a blow-by-blow account from memory, including:
1. what happened chronologically;
2. what they thought was happening and what they did as a result;
3. what they felt at different stages throughout the session. This account is then given to the supervisor to study and is used as the focus of a later supervision session.

Circumstances. We think it should be used sparingly in a placement. It has a particular value where a supervisor is having difficulty in getting a very full account of a student's work from discussion or from case records.

Advantages. It is still the only method of supervision which gives the supervisor systematic access to the thoughts and feelings of the student as they are formulated in the course of their work, and their relationship to the student's actions in the intervention. It requires no equipment, it is within the control of the student, and it is a model of what practitioners need to achieve in the ordinary course of their work, i.e. a degree of consciousness about the process of their intervention. They need to be able to achieve this objective if they are to develop self-awareness in their work and not be too unconscious of their actions.

Disadvantages. It could perhaps create hyper-self-consciousness in a student who may be self-conscious already, e.g. a student in the stage of acute self-consciousness described by Reynolds (1965). It may be considered laborious and time-consuming for those students who are not used to examining their thoughts and feelings, or who dislike writing. If the supervisor does not subsequently make creative use of the information that is provided, there is a danger of setting up an aversion to this method of supervision in the student, as there will not have been a proportionate pay-off in learning for the student from the effort invested in it. It is an unfashionable method at the present time, being associated with the psycho-dynamic approach to working with clients. This is a pity, because all interventions in social work require self-awareness on the part of workers and a sensitivity to the feelings, attitudes and behaviour of other people.

Knowledge and skills. Because of the demands made on the student, this method places a greater responsibility on supervisors to prepare adequately from the material provided. They should remember that:
1. it is a descriptive narrative;
2. the student is not encouraged to analyse abstractly from it;
3. the aim is to try to get at a student's processes of thinking, feeling and acting;
4. they should try to identify as many possible issues in the accounts, for example the dynamics – the feelings, roles, cultural patterns etc. that are taking place in the interview:

defences against anxiety or feelings; and reflection which seems to be going on.

Before the session begins supervisors should allow their own feelings to engage the experiences being recounted, to help them to empathise with the feelings which the student still has subsequent to the intervention. In the session itself, it would be sensible to begin with those issues that the supervisor feels that the student understands or is near to understanding from the sense of the narrative. They should be tentative, so that the supervisor can choose whether to withdraw from any material which may be too worrying for the student. They should ensure that they can explain why they have made a particular connection and, furthermore, why understanding the particular connection is valuable in the work with the client.

The supervisor should look for patterns, rather than risk labouring an isolated issue, which even if it is correct can get the discussion bogged down in resistance and misunderstanding. It is useful to ask the student what he or she feels was important about the interview – the facts, the dynamics, and any strong feelings that emerge during the course of it; also to discover the student's feelings after a period of reflection.

The use of video tape

In this method the student videotapes an interview or part-interview or a piece of intervention and then makes the recording available to the supervisor as a basis for discussion in supervision. The video camera may be taken to the client's home, or it may be used in an office or any situation where the student's work is normally undertaken.

Star (1977) has demonstrated experimentally in a laboratory setting the impact of videotape performance on student self-images as helpers. Rhim (1976) describes the use of video on an agency and its benefits: supervision, self-learning by staff, and the positive impact on clients. Meltzer (1977) gives an account of a joint collaboration between a social work course and two agencies, to produce videotapes of work with clients for teaching purposes, including work by students. Howard and Gooderham (1975) describe the use of video in role play exercises with social work students, with the aim of extending the students' sensitivity and skills with clients.

Circumstances. Videotape may be helpfully used in any situation in which it is feasible to take the equipment. At the same time it can also be used as a method of feedback to clients on how they deal with their problems, relate to other people, or as a method of acquiring personal problem-solving skills. For the purposes of learning for the student, the emphasis will be on the interaction between the student and the client, or others, and their skill in the approach being used. The supervisor may introduce it as a method of supervision in the placement simply because it is available. It is a useful tool for self-learning for any student. Further than this, it can give the supervisor a detailed, blow-by-blow access to the student's work, without the presence of a third party, unless someone is necessary for camera shots. It also offers the facility of 'action replays'.

Advantages. Videotape gives a 'camera-doesn't-lie' source of evidence for the student's performance for the purposes of evaluation, as well as for the value of self-learning to the student. It provides immediate, accurate, detailed and sustained feedback on performance. The tape can be stored and referred to again in a leisurely way, as a source of reference for comparison with later performance.

Disadvantages. While the camera doesn't 'lie', it does not convey the whole truth. It tends to 'flatten out' emotions and the subtleties of communication, and, of course, those outside the range of a camera will be lost. Thus the video recorder is not a substitute for trained personal observation, nor for the responsibility on the part of students to communicate their understanding of their work. Hopefully these will be congruent with each other.

'Trial by video' may be regarded as daunting by some students, although others may welcome the opportunity to go in front of a camera. The consent of clients and others must be carefully negotiated, assurances given about the proper purposes of the recording, and safeguards offered with regard to future use and possible audiences. While the use of video tape has increasingly become normal practice in some agencies, particularly family therapy centres, it can be onerous to set up in some circumstances, and it may constrain spontaneity because of the technical procedures that need to be followed.

Knowledge and skills. As with other 'technical' methods of supervision, the use of videotape is only as good as the benefits that are gained from it for the purposes of supervision. The more exacting it is in exposing the detail of the student's performance in the intervention being taped, the more exacting it can be in the explicitness it may demand from a supervisor in offering feedback on performance. It is probably wise from the beginning not to set up unjustified expectations that the feedback from a single intervention will provide either comprehensive evidence of the quality of a student's performance or unambiguous feedback on the student's skill in approach or the method being used. It is more likely to provide the latter if a methodologically distinct approach is being used, e.g. structural family therapy.

As with other methods, it is preferable to keep the responsibility for learning with the student as far as and for as long as possible. While the supervisor should view the tape prior to the supervision session, students should be asked to prepare a presentation on what they think the main learning issues are on the basis of the tape. Only after the exposition is completed should the supervisor intervene, indeed if this is necessary at all. The student can halt the play-back to clarify issues and emphasise points of learning. Hair-splitting and over-concern with detail is usually best avoided. Only when there are substantial issues, perhaps on matters of principle or where important propositions related to methodology are at stake, should the supervisor take the student back over the tape. Hopefully, the evidence to support the contention will be available on the tape recording and, where necessary, reference can be made to written texts which illustrate and support the point of view.

The use of audio

Understandably much of what has been written about the use of videotape has relevance to the use of audio recording as a method of teaching and learning. Audio recorders may be used in the office, home or in any setting for the purpose of self-learning or for evaluation of performance by the supervisor.

Circumstances. The audio recorder is suitable for use by the student as an adjunct to other methods of teaching and learning and to refer to in reviewing any aspects of their spoken interaction with clients or others. A supervisor may wish to encourage its use in order to gain a more detailed, first-hand access to the interaction between the student and client or others involved in helping, e.g. volunteers.

Advantages. These are the same as for the use of a video recording, but with the added advantage that audio recorders are usually smaller, more portable, less dependent on accessories such as decent lighting, and even independent of mains power. A further advantage is that they are in ready supply.

Disadvantages. On first consideration the tape recorder seems a much more limited facility than, say, a video tape. Its use is dependent on a 'visual' briefing by the student, in the form of a description of the setting, the seating arrangements and pen-pictures of the participants. However, the listener is not then distracted by the 'movement' in a video presentation, which can take attention away from conversation, the process of discussion, the subtleties of exchange and the tone of feeling between the participants. While silences and non-verbal interaction are not available to the listener, this need not detract too much from the value of the recording. It is surprising how valuable it can be to 'listen' to a videotape recording without the presence of the picture.

Knowledge and skills. These are similar to those described in the use of videotape recording, and as with other methods should be seen in conjunction with the general approach to teaching and learning which we have advocated for all the methods being used.

7

Methods of Teaching and Learning (II)

Group supervision

In the main, student supervision tends to be a one-to-one activity: the opportunities for learning are managed by and limited to one supervisor. We have tried to emphasise that having a student on placement requires a team approach, so that colleagues can offer additional opportunities for learning and wider perspectives on the student's performance. Group supervision further enlarges the concept of supervision. A group offers greater variety of experience to each participant and therefore offers the greatest potential for learning. There is research evidence that 'substantial economies in field instructor time could be achieved through use of group supervision methods' (Sales and Navarre, (1970).

Description. To date, little has been published on group supervision, although it has been practised for some years, particularly in student units. Sales and Navarre offer an interesting comparison of individual supervision and group supervision. Davis (1977) in her selection of papers on 'student group supervision' defines it as 'a regular pattern of focused discussion, shared between fieldwork teacher(s) and two or more supervisees'. Another definition describes it as the process of 'group problem solving'.

There are a number of models of group supervision that can be used:

1. A group of students and a practice teacher who conducts all aspects of supervision, including individual assess-

ments, in the group. This model obviously has implications for evaluation and assessment, as the supervisor's assessments presumably have to be open to the views of others. It might be appropriate, therefore, to seek the views of the student, the other students and other supervisors if applicable, while the main supervisor remains responsible for collating the views and takes the final responsibility for the conclusion of the assessment.

2. A group of students supervised individually by their practice teachers, but also meeting as a group with their practice teacher(s) for some supervision. This should probably more correctly be called 'group teaching' or 'group consultation' rather than supervision, which incorporates the responsibility for evaluation and assessment.

3. The opportunity for the student to participate, with or without the supervisor, in a staff group, for example a fostering support group.

4. Where a student has been co-working on a case or project, group supervision could entail just the two workers with the designated supervisor for that particular piece of work.

In the same way that there are various models of group supervision, the focus for discussion in the group can also be varied. It need not only be problem-focused or used to discuss or review cases being worked on by the participants. The following are a number of alternatives:

1. Participants might present a particular topic for discussion, perhaps a method of working, or an issue that has emerged in their work.

2. They might discuss a piece of legislation or an article on a particular subject.

3. The group might be supervising a member(s) on a project in which they are involved.

4. The group leader might introduce 'games' to increase self-awareness and sensitivity.

5. They may wish to discuss the value of different teaching/learning techniques, for example, role-playing or the use of audio or visual tapes, co-working, etc.

6. The group might want to role-play a potentially threatening group situation, for example a case conference or court appearance.

Circumstances. Although to our knowledge group super-vision has been mainly developed in student units, it can be used in any placement setting where a member of students are placed simultaneously. It should not be a deterrent that the students are all placed with different supervisors: as pre-viously described, a number of students with their respective supervisors might come together, or one or two supervisors may be designated to lead group sessions in addition to individual supervision. In community work placements or where there are a number of students placed together in a day centre or residential placement, and thus working with the same clients, group supervision will be particularly appropri-ate.

Advantages. There is a number of clear advantages to using this particular method of teaching and learning:

1. Experiences can be shared in a way which enables members to learn from a number of others, providing a greater variety of information on any subject and an opportunity to examine concepts from different perspec-tives. Students benefit from relating previous experiences to the present task, and therefore learn from each other's previous experiences. This applies to both students and supervisors.

2. There is less chance of supervisors inappropriately impos-ing their own values, methods, preconceptions, even prejudices, on a student. Sales and Navarre found that students in group supervision felt greater freedom to communicate dissatisfactions with 'field instruction' to their supervisors, and greater freedom to differ with them about professional ideas.

3. In a case of personality conflict between a student and supervisor the group may be able to contribute towards resolving the conflict. One member of the group may be able to express the difficulty, of which the supervisor might be unaware, on behalf of another group member. Criticism from a fellow student may be more acceptable than from the supervisor. At the very least, group supervision can provide a continuing and more positive learning experience to a student who may be getting an

inadequate service from the supervisor.

4. It offers students the possibility of a greater measure of responsibility for their own learning. Within the group, roles change and students will have opportunities to occupy a variety of roles, including that of teacher to other students.

5. Group supervision has an additional advantage in that it provides an opportunity for students to increase their understanding of group dynamics and to enhance their ability to cope with the many group situations in which they may find themselves in their work, for example working with families or initiating self-help groups.

Disadvantages. The disadvantages are as follows:

1. Students may sometimes feel that their own personal needs are not being met because of the needs of others. For example, a group member with extensive learning difficulties may take up a disproportionate amount of the group's energies. In selecting members for supervision groups, it may be sensible to exclude students who are vulnerable in this way.

2. The supervision group may emphasise differences in ability and thereby prevent learning. Some students and supervisors may feel inhibited in sharing their supervisory relationship with others, for example in a group where a number of students and their supervisors join together. Normally supervisors are in a position where their skills are not easily measured and thus they are not easily threatened by others. The supervisor in a group situation may fear the loss of this protection.

3. Students may feel that expressing their ignorance and lack of confidence to one supervisor is bad enough, without having to do it in a group. Another disadvantage could be that if group sessions replace individual sessions entirely, the student might lose out by not having any single person to whom they can relate, and who is primarily responsible for ensuring that their learning needs are met.

4. There is a tendency in supervision groups to concentrate on problems rather than more positive aspects of learning. Thus solutions are sometimes elusive, so impetus can flag

and participants lose interest. Without competent leadership, members can get stuck in roles. An articulate,
opinionated member might tend to dominate the discussion; on the other hand, a less confident member or a lazy
one may cease to participate. The leader, perhaps because
of anxiety about the group's progress, may be too directive
or may tend to monopolise the discussion.

Knowledge and skills. It is important for the practice teacher
to recognise the change in roles from individual supervisor to
group leader. One of the dangers for the inexperienced leader
is that instead of group supervision taking place, individual
supervision will take place in a group setting. Providing an
initial structure would be one of the leadership functions of
the practice teacher, while at the same time aiming at
agreement about the purposes of the group and a shared
responsibility for decision-making. Developing further the
idea of 'contracts' in practice placements, the aim might be to
establish a contract for the group. It would cover issues such
as membership, commitment, frequency and length of sessions, time-keeping, the purpose and content of sessions, the
responsibilities of members, and the responsibility for chairing and evaluation. An important issue would be how much
criticism members would want or feel that they could cope
with in the group.

In any small working group, the leader has two primary
functions: (a) encouraging the achievement of goals; and (b)
facilitating effective working relationships within the group.

Whilst encouraging other group members to take over
aspects of the leadership function, the practice teacher/leader
is ultimately responsible for:
1. Structuring group supervision, that is clarifying the aims
   and organising the sessions.
2. Assessing the learning needs of the members and maxi-
   mising learning opportunities for individuals.
3. Encouraging members to participate and to share the
   teaching role.
4. Evaluating progress.
In contemplating a move into group supervision, the practice
teacher will need to have achieved a level of competence in

individual supervision. Ideally it would be helpful if the practice teacher had previous experience of being a member of a learning group and thus had the opportunity to learn something of the processes of groups. As with individual supervision, the practice teacher will need to have some knowledge and understanding of how adults learn. Furthermore, they will need knowledge of how small groups function, for example the composition of effective groups, types of leadership, patterns of communication, and stages of group development.

Role playing and modelling in supervision

Description. Role-playing is being used when the participants attempt to portray a situation as if it were real, using their knowledge and experience to convey how they think the person they are role-playing would behave, think and feel. It is not the same as acting, because the role players do not follow a prepared script; they have the freedom to develop the role as they think appropriate, probably in the context of an agreed role-set.

The great value in using role play for teaching in a placement is that it enables students to practise their social work skills in a simulated situation.

Modelling goes on indirectly all the time in a placement: a student sharing a room with colleagues will learn and copy their telephone responses; or when accompanying colleagues on visits will be learning how to deal with different situations, in a similar way to any apprentice learning his/her trade. However, it can also be used in a more direct way.

There are a number of ways in which these methods can be used:

1. *For rehearsal*: the student can rehearse how a particular interview might be dealt with, for example an initial visit. Different approaches could be rehearsed in order to determine the most appropriate. Any potentially anxiety-provoking situation can be rehearsed in the same way, for example presenting a court report or attending a case conference. In a similar way students can be encouraged to test out their ability to deal with difficult behaviour, for

example aggression or rejection, in the safety of the supervision session.

2. *For demonstration*: where a student is asking for direct guidance on how to handle a particular situation, the supervisor, using a combination of role-play and modelling, may show the student different strategies. As well as being offered suggestions, the student, in role-playing a client, would gain insight into a client's feelings.

3. *For micro-teaching of social work skills*: Carpenter and Deschrer (1982) describe the more sophisticated use of role play in the course of teaching family therapy skills. The essential feature in this method of teaching is the repeated rehearsals of therapist skills by using role play in a small group. A skill is initially demonstrated by the teacher, and then the practice performances of the students are evaluated, providing a useful method of assessing student skills. Carpenter and Deschrer argue that 'the general increase in confidence to use family therapy skills as a result of preparing the role play, indicated the potential of videotape role plays as an educational as well as assessment device'. This micro-teaching model was developed by Ivey and colleagues (Ivey *et al.*, 1968; Ivey and Authier, 1975) and was originally designed for teaching individual counselling skills.

4. *With clients*: a student might use similar techniques with clients, either in one-to-one situations or, for example, in a social skills group. A client could be given the opportunity to rehearse attendance at court or a tribunal, or a meeting with the head teacher. By using a combination of role play and modelling, the student could suggest strategies for dealing with these various situations. Another use might be to reverse roles with a client, using this opportunity to offer insight to the client as to their own behaviour and the feelings they create in others. This could also be done with a co-worker, for example in marital counselling.

Circumstances. Traditionally, role play has been used for learning purposes in social work training by constructing elaborate 'sets', for example court scenes and compulsory mental health admissions. Not unexpectedly, students have expressed criticisms of this method of teaching, complaining that the scenarios are unrealistic and that self-consciousness and nervousness about 'performing' negates the learning that can be derived from it. However, we would suggest that role play, used frequently and often spontaneously in either individual supervision or small groups, can provide a valuable alternative as part of the practice teacher's repertoire of teaching methods.

It is difficult to separate role play from modelling, as in many instances of role play there is also the opportunity to learn through colleagues' performances. The use of video to film role plays adds a further dimension to learning in that it offers students the opportunity to observe themselves and evaluate their own performance. (See Chapter 6 on the use of video tape.)

Advantages
1. Role play provides the practice teacher with the opportunity to observe directly the student performing; if used
   regularly, as in the micro-teaching model, evaluation of
   the student's progress in learning skills is possible. By
   taking the client's role, the practice teacher is able to feed
   back to the student their effect on the client, so that the
   student also receives evaluation from the 'role-play client'.
2. Role-playing enables students to test out in safety their
   anxieties and fears about what they anticipate will be
   threatening clients or situations. It enables the student to
   become more self-aware.
3. Exposure on the part of both supervisor and student
   enhances the notion of mutual learning. The degree of
   learning will be directly related to the degree of trust and
   safety that has developed in the relationship.
4. In using role play to practise skills, the student is acquiring
   another interventive technique to offer clients.
Role play is a flexible and therefore useful method of teaching. The basic method that we describe is readily available to any supervisor and student: it demands no equipment and very little preparation, and it can be used in any placement setting. It needs to be used frequently, as a

regular feature of supervision, so that the novelty does not interfere with the learning.

Disadvantages

1. Unless role play is used frequently it can generate a degree of self-consciousness which will inhibit learning. There might be students who find the idea of role playing too threatening even to try it.

2. If an interview is rehearsed and then the 'real-life' interview does not develop along similar lines, this can cause anxiety for students because they might not have reached the stage where they can adjust their approach flexibly. Similarly, in trying to conduct the actual interview in the way it was previously rehearsed, the student could be unreceptive or insensitive to other issues that emerge. It might be best to have a time-lag between the rehearsal and the performance, so that the student has a chance to assimilate the learning.

3. To avoid discouragement on the part of the student, modelling which is demonstrated by the supervisor must not be too far beyond a standard attainable by the student. Modelling in a planned way to demonstrate skills is perhaps more appropriate to a student at an early stage of their learning. It is therefore particularly important that the practice teacher, as an experienced practitioner, is aware of the gap between the standard of their performance and that of the student.

4. One of the difficulties that Carpenter and Deschrer experienced in teaching family therapy skills was the tendency for 'role-play clients/families' to lapse into inauthentic behaviour. This no doubt contributes to the criticism that role play is unrealistic.

Knowledge and skills. It is important to allow students who are participating in a role play the opportunity to comment on and evaluate their performance as soon as possible afterwards, so that feelings aroused by it do not get lost or blurred by a time-lag and thus lose their learning value. The practice teacher needs to be aware that role play can be threatening to students and that appreciation of their efforts and positive feedback are needed quickly. Sensitivity is important here, as role play is such an immediate medium of teaching and there is no opportunity for considered evaluation. It is helpful if the practice teacher is reasonably unselfconscious, offering a model to the student. The initiative to use role play as a method will need to come from the supervisor, who must feel confident that this is an effective method of teaching.

Co-working

Description. This method involves a supervisor and student intentionally working together on a case or project, as a method of enhancing the student's learning. Co-working tends to arise naturally or unavoidably in residential or day-care settings, where social workers help the residents as a team, often working co-operatively and in full view of each other. The student in this setting is often co-working with their supervisor as a matter of necessity.

A form of co-working which is increasingly developing in social work agencies is where staff have developed a team approach to intervening in families. This occurs where the other members of the team act as consultants to the social worker working directly with the family. A supervisor may be a member of the team acting as a consultant to a student or indeed a student may be in that capacity to the supervisor. Schlenoff and Busa (1981) describe the value of co-working by a student and a supervisor in a setting in which group work is the chosen method of helping. They not only describe the value of this method of learning but also techniques for dealing with the imbalance of power between the co-workers. In their experience, co-working in placements is not uncommon, but it is unclear whether it is chosen for the purpose of teaching the student or because the method or client group is one of mutual interest.

Circumstances. Setting aside for a moment the opportunism involved in using the method in settings where it is unavoidable in the nature of the work or in the method of support, practice teachers can usefully examine the pros and cons of using it in a setting where it would be the method of deliberate choice.

Schlenoff and Busa (1981) see it as arising out of the apprenticeship model of training and utilise it in a group work setting where two workers would always be used with a group. Presumably a practice teacher would only use the method where it was appropriate to have two workers involved. On that basis it could be used in any situation where two workers were needed, where the student was to acquire the skills, and where the supervisor had these particular skills to offer.

Because of the unequal nature of the supervisor/student relationship we would caution against use of this method where concern was already felt by the supervisor about the capabilities of the student. The student would be in the invidious situation of being an unequal partner in relation to the practice and feeling under a degree of scrutiny which was likely to inhibit his or her confidence even further.

Co-working in a placement need not involve the supervisor so directly; the co-worker could be a colleague. The responsibility for work supervision can be delegated to that co-worker, or, more preferably the placement supervisor can act as a supervisor/consultant to the total co-working partnership.

Advantages. Co-working has the obvious advantage for the student of direct learning through the demonstration of skills by the more experienced co-worker. It also presents the student with professional support and precise feedback on performance arising out of the discussions which should take place in the debriefing session afterwards. It provides immediate and direct learning which can be offered by few other methods of teaching. Schlenoff and Busa (1981) argue that it makes training shorter and more effective.

Disadvantages. Setting aside for a moment the issue of the supervisor being the co-worker, this method can make it hard for the supervisor to disentangle the separate contributions of each co-worker and to be sure about what has been learned independently by the student. For their part, students may be overwhelmed by the greater experience of the co-worker and forced into a passive role in both action and discussion, possibly losing rather than increasing their confidence.

A further problem is created for the student if the co-worker is their supervisor. Some would argue that co-working is in any case better carried out by equally competent contributors (Yallom, 1969), but in the case of the supervisor there are additional levels of inequality and authority to be disentangled. Is the student free to challenge the authority of the more experienced partner, and if they do, is it a challenge to the supervisor's expertise, his or her competence in the agency, or the delegated responsibility from the course? Similarly, is the supervisor, when offering teaching or criticism, speaking as a more experienced peer, the protector of agency standards or the assessor of standards on behalf of the course? It is argued that these complexities can be overcome by incorporating particular techniques of working into the knowledge and skills of the method (Schlenoff and Busa, 1981).

Knowledge and skills. In addition to teaching the knowledge and skills required for the work itself, supervisors must be able to take into account the additional ones that are necessary to deal with the unequal power relationship between themselves and the students. It will be helpful if they are prepared from the beginning to emphasise the value of the different perspectives which students are able to bring, despite their relative inexperience. Furthermore, they must be willing to take the initiative to open themselves up to being critically questioned by their students. It will be helpful if they invite students to offer their opinions first, so that students' opinions are not overwhelmed by those which derive from the greater experience of supervisors. Supervisors should encourage students to offer their opinions, support them in principle, and handle disagreements in a sensitive way. It is vital that they engage in pre- and post-session discussions, so that any difficulties that arise can be dealt with in the course of the work. It might be helpful to use a consultant, who can help supervisors not only to understand the work that is going on in the sessions, but also to disentangle any relationship difficulties which inevitably develop in such close working relationships. This can lend objectivity to the work and act as a corrective to supervisors who may at times have difficulty in objectively separating students' performances from the feelings that can be aroused in these relationships. It is crucial that sufficient confidence is developed in these relationships for criticisms to be voiced openly. The main responsibility for ensuring that this occurs lies with supervisors.

8

Learning, Learning Problems and the Problematic Learner

The aim of this chapter is to introduce the supervisor to a range of ideas, concepts and approaches which we think will be useful in recognising learning difficulties and helping the student to overcome them. Students commonly experience a variety of learning difficulties, from the more frequent very minor ones, which the supervisor might decide to 'write off', to the less common, more serious ones, which might lead to consideration of failing. Learning problems do not come neatly packaged, but often emerge gradually in the form of 'symptoms'. Often they are readily owned by the student, who brings them to supervision for help, but sometimes they have to be 'proved' by the practice teacher.

Any learning is invariably something of a problem to a student, and the supervisor needs a range of understandings about the nature of ordinary learning and about difficulties in problem-solving, which we call learning problems. Very occasionally there will be a student with exceptional learning difficulties, amounting sometimes to what has been called the 'ineducable learner' (Towle, 1954), and we examine criteria which the supervisor might utilise in considering the question of failing.

Perspectives on learning

In the following sections we intend to introduce the work of a number of specialists in methods of and problems in professional learning, which we feel would be helpful to the practice teacher. Their work covers the process of learning, anxieties and fears in learning, and approaches to overcoming learning problems.

Some models of learning

Leslie Button's (1971) model suggests a conceptualisation of the process of learning which is relevant to supervisors:
1. The first stage is to help the student to an intellectual grasp of the theoretical principles. Button suggests that this is not too difficult. For example, in using crisis theory, the principles involved are that:
   (a) help should be offered at the time the crisis develops;
   (b) it should be focused on supporting the coping capacities of the client; and
   (c) the emphasis should be on encouragement, helpfulness and the provision of practical environmental resources.
2. In order to be useful, the new theoretical material has to be integrated into the student's existing insights, that is, into a personal framework of understanding. In the case of crisis theory, this will partly depend on the student's experience of crisis or crisis work and thus on whether the idea 'makes sense'.
3. The knowledge may not become operational as a usable tool until it has been practised several times. Presumably a placement will offer a number of opportunities for crisis intervention during which the efficacy of the idea can be tested and evaluated in action.
4. The student's personal attributes will play a part in this process of learning: intellectual capacities, openness to new ideas, courage and determination to put new ideas into practice, or in dealing with familiar situations in new ways.

Thus, in this model of learning, students need to understand the nature of the social worker's role as a generalisation while at the same time developing their own style of responding to any given situation. In relation to the overall learning in the placement, it will be important for the supervisor to have a clear idea of what the student is to learn.

An alternative learning model suggests the following steps or sequence of thinking towards the solution of a learning problem:

1. The student faces a difficulty or a question which cannot be answered at the present time.
2. The next step is to identify the problem more clearly by analysis, e.g. collecting relevant facts and reasoning about them in relation to the problem at hand.
3. Formulating possible hypotheses, i.e. possible explanations or alternative solutions to the problem. At this stage students will frequently be able to draw upon generalisations or principles they already know about. It will be part of the practice teacher's role to contribute to the provision of reliable principles, propositions or theories which may be considered to be appropriate.
4. Students then test the hypothesis by appropriate means, through the experience of helping.
5. Drawing conclusions, i.e. hopefully solving the problem.

Inductive and deductive approaches to learning by students

The two models outlined above are examples of deductive and inductive approaches to learning respectively. In the first model, by Button, the student is utilising the deductive approach to learning by applying an already existing hypothesis or method to a problem, for which it would already claim to be a solution. The deductive learner is someone who characteristically prefers to apply a theory or method to problems.

The second model uses the inductive approach to learning and describes a process whereby the person approaches a problem without a set solution to it and goes about examining it, collecting information, attempting to understand and to classify it and then draws on information already known to them which would claim not only to throw light on it, but provide guidance towards a solution. Someone who characteristically uses this approach to learning and problem-solving can be described as an inductive learner.

Some crucial conditions for learning

In addition to understanding the process, or sequence of steps, through which students learn, it is helpful for practice teachers to be aware of what Miller (1966) has described as 'conditions for learning'. By this he does not mean physical facilities or amenities, but propensities in the learner or the learning situation, over which the supervisor and the student have some control, which must be present if effective learning is to take place. These conditiions are held to apply whether the student inclines to an inductive or deductive learning approach, and in whichever kind of placement setting the student is located. They are in a sense generic elements for student learning. They have been described as follows:

Adequate motivation for learning. This may have little to do with the desire to learn in itself, but is a factor which leads to resistance and lack of involvement on the part of the learner, e.g. fear of failure, discomfort about change, etc. This can be overcome
1. by making the learning relevant to the student's life pattern;
2. by making it feel satisfying;
3. by influencing the learning group; the group must matter to individual members, it must be a cohesive group; and it must develop shared values which are hospitable to educational change in the desired direction.
Motivation ought not to be a problem for social work students, who have after all made a commitment to following a particular vocational course, and it is generally felt not to be the responsibility of teachers to motivate the learner. Ideally, this factor should be dealt with during selection.

Awareness of the inadequacy of the student's present behaviour. The major resistance to change in the context of adult learning is the defensiveness aroused on behalf of already established behaviours. The student requires sufficient security to be able to relax any defensive posture. With regard to the existing attitudes held by the student, these must be accepted by the supervisor, even if they are not agreed with.

A clear picture of the behaviours which a student is to adopt. In social work we may want a student to acquire a way of learning, rather than merely a specific learning goal. There are elements of modelling which take place implicitly and explicitly, and the practice teacher may need to introduce a clear picture of the behaviours which the learner is expected to adopt. Students do not always 'catch on' through the activities alone.

Opportunities to practise the appropriate behaviours. Students must have opportunities to be active in some appropriate fashion if they are to have the opportunity to acquire what they are supposed to learn. A practice placement is the ideal situation for students to practice appropriate behaviours.

Reinforcement of the correct behaviour. Students must get feedback as continuously as possible about their progress or lack of progress in their work.

The student must have available the sequence of appropriate materials. The 'materials' in the context of social work education and training refer to workload, projects, reading, etc. They must not only be comprehensible and appropriate to the abilities of the student, but their purposes must be made clear in relation to the personal learning goals of the student. It is particularly important that students are not asked to undertake work that is far beyond their capacities at the present moment, which we acknowledge is much more difficult to achieve in actual practice.

Normal learning fears and anxieties

Towle (1954) suggests that there are some understandable anxieties and fears for the student which are inherent to social work education:
1. Fear of helplessness due to (a) lack of knowledge, and (b)

dealing with the time-lag between what has been taught
and the ability to put it into practice.
2. Fear related to high expectations of self or out of concern
for those being served.
3. Fear of the new by reason of its nature and meaning,
rather than fear of the newness itself.
4. When the integrative task exceeds the integrative capacity, the learner often erects defences against anxiety,
which impede rather than support learning. These concepts are useful in relation to a student's learning. The
integrative task is the total of learning which the student
has to accomplish at any one time in a placement. In total
this would be all the learning planned for the placement
and should ideally be a little ahead of the student's
integrative capacity if it is to produce a stimulating learning
experience. The integrative capacity of the student is his or
her ability to accomplish the learning to the level required
of the placement.

The integrative task and the integrative capacity may at times
be temporarily out of joint during the placement. It is not
always possible for a supervisor to judge the degree to which
the student is able to absorb new learning and to put it into
practice or to provide learning challenges at the pace and
level that is suited to the student. When this lack of matching
occurs, at worst it is likely only to cause temporary boredom
or stress for the student. However, if the integrative task is
pitched correctly and the student persistently fails to accomplish it, then this will be a matter of concern and will raise the
question of failing.

Overcoming learning problems

Most ordinary learning problems can be dealt with within the
following approach, involving four stages:

Identification of the problem. It may be the student who
brings the difficulty to the supervisor's attention in the first
place. If this is not the case, then the supervisor must be

precise about what the problem is considered to be and what evidence, i.e. what behaviour, leads them to this conclusion. Sometimes the supervisor may feel concerned, but find it difficult to make it explicit. Translating such concern into evidence, which the student might be able to recognise and acknowledge, can be a difficult process for supervisors and an aspect of supervision in which they might well need support from their own line manager or perhaps from a peer support group, if this is available.

Recognition by the student. It is important that students recognise the problem themselves, in order that they are motivated to do something about it. This potentially can be threatening for students, as they may have to challenge some previous learning in order to take on board the possibilities of new learning.

Agreement on ways of overcoming the difficulties. One of the most important skills for the social work student to learn is that of problem-solving. Students approach problem-solving differently. Some must be taught step-by-step procedures to analyse a problem and then to work out a solution. Others are often able to make larger mental jumps. Supervisors are justified in expecting that students should be able to apply the same problem-solving process to their own learning difficulties that they would apply in tackling problems with clients or other work tasks.

If, for example, a student lacks knowledge on a particular topic or of resources available, then the agreed way of tackling this might be for the supervisor to suggest specific reading that the student should undertake within a time limit. The supervisor might also suggest sources of information for the student. If a student has a difficulty in his or her style of writing, then the agreed way of tackling this might be for the supervisor and student to take a thorough look at all letters written over the following week.

To look for evidence of the difficulty having been overcome. If the student is in a similar situation in the future, has their ability to deal with the problem improved and therefore are they well on the way to resolving the difficulty? Or have they apparently been unable to integrate the new learning and therefore repeated the same inappropriate behaviour? If supervisors are able to identify evidence of learning progress, it is important that they acknowledge it with positive reinforcement of the improved behaviour.

We know that students do not learn at an even pace, but that learning ebbs and flows depending on such factors as familiarity with problems, the stress involved, the personal circumstances of the student, etc. In general terms the supervisor will need to distinguish between problems in learning and the problem learner. It is important to provide the student with critical feedback, and it should be given quickly. Although this is a major responsibility of the supervisor, at the same time the supervisor needs to be aware of the vulnerability of the student and to ensure that criticism is not destructive. The supervisor should avoid evoking compliance in a learner or offer so much criticism at any one time that it leads to loss of confidence. Criticism should be related to particular learning and performance behaviours, rather than directed to the personality of the learner. However in the end, responsibility for learning must be the student's. Also, if students are not able to make the learning their own, then they will not be able to apply it with conviction in an integrated way. In the end, any learning difficulty will be resolved in one of the following ways:

1. it will be overcome;
2. it will be written off against all the other good work the student has been able to accomplish;
3. it will be passed on clearly in the placement report, with the student's knowledge, to the next placement.
4. it will be serious enough to warrant consideration of failing the placement.

In practice, it is unlikely that a student will fail a placement on any one item of performance, as failing is usually the result of more generalised learning difficulties.

Some examples of common learning difficulties and helpful responses

Anxiety

As we stated earlier, all learning is something of a worry, but some learning problems create anxiety in students. Crisis theory has taught us of the nature and value of 'worry work' (Caplan, 1961), and this is the usual, constructive approach of students to learning problems. However, if worry extends into anxiety, it becomes a problem, especially if students show signs of being inhibited by it into inactivity – for example, when they cannot get themselves to make a visit to clients or make a phone call; when they constantly report back on their every action; or when they plan in great detail for every visit.

It is helpful to acknowledge the feelings and to give permission to the student to be anxious. The supervisor needs to set limited goals that are well within the student's capacities, so that in achieving these the student gains confidence. The visits and meetings can be rehearsed at supervision sessions by using role play. (This has been discussed in detail in Chapter 7.) The student will need reassurance and lots of positive reinforcement if this can be appropriately given. Sometimes anxiety can be a much more serious problem, and we discuss this later in this chapter.

Difficulty in producing written work

The student might acknowledge difficulty in keeping records up to date or in knowing what to write in a report. The supervisor might feel concerned about the quality of the written work produced or might have become exasperated by the student's frequent excuses for not producing required written work on time.

There can be a variety of causes of problems in producing written work. Students might not be clear as to what is required, particularly if the placement setting is not one with which they are familiar. It is useful to discuss the purpose of recording with students in order that they understand the different types of recording that will be acceptable in different circumstances. Some students find it difficult to expose their written work to the possibility of criticism; some have difficulty in conceptualising generally; some have been inhibited by having too high expectations of themselves and are continually dissatisfied with their efforts; others are just lazy! The supervisor might involve the tutor in finding out the extent to which a student has difficulty in producing written work for the course. Is it a general problem or is it specific to this work or this placement? The supervisor might introduce the idea of a 'day book' in which the student can keep daily notes of his or her activities and then use it as a basis for recording when this is required. Students must have time allowed for recording purposes. They need to have realistic deadlines and a clear idea of the purpose of their records. It is important to try to overcome the difficulty in the placement, as this can become a chronic problem in future work. For example:

> J, a relatively experienced student, wrote records which were both too long and which failed to identify either the important aspects of interviews or his own position. The supervisor requested that future recording items should be no longer than ten lines and should indicate the conclusions drawn. This strategy liberated the student to write more concise, expressive and analytical records.

The way in which students learn to record in the practice placement is likely to be carried forward in their future professional work. It is important to help them to differentiate between recording for the purposes of supervision and recording for the purposes of the agency records. Practice teachers will need to be aware of the current debate on clients' access to their records and of its possible impact on a student's skill in recording. Process recording, or detailed information gathered for assessment work, might be appropriate for a first placement student or for the purposes of student supervision, but it is not appropriate for leaving in the agency file.

Students need to be helped to distinguish between fact and opinion, the importance of accurate records, the value of confidentiality, and the power of invalid records possibly to disadvantage the interests of clients. In a final placement, the supervisor may appropriately spend time in encouraging the student to become skilled in recognising what information is needed for agency purposes.

Dealing with aggression

Students are often concerned about how they will handle this particular type of behaviour in a client. If a student has come to associate excessive anxiety with aggression in other people, then anxiety that will impede the work with the client is likely to be a feature in these situations. It may lead to avoidance of such situations on the part of the student or to aggressive responses to the client out of feelings of defensiveness. Awareness of these responses through supervision will normally lead to greater control of the feelings by being able to anticipate them. Another way in which control can be achieved is through 'desensitisation', i.e. through gradually learning to be less anxious in the actual situation by developing more responsive skills with increasingly aggressive clients. Using role play in supervision is also a useful method for allowing the student to practise new skills and strategies in dealing with this form of behaviour.

Avoiding supervision

Charlotte Towle gives an example of a student who has bungled two cases through not seeking appropriate supervision. Although self-condemning and remorseful, the student nonetheless repeated the omission. In the discussion which followed, the supervisor conveyed a willingness to understand, while making the focus for concern the resulting failure of the service to clients. In attempting to reconstruct the reason which led to the decision not to consult, it transpired that the student felt a sense of failure at having to seek help. Initially, following the discussion, the student tended to over-consult, but gradually developed a more balanced and appropriate level of autonomy and dependence.

The 'independent' student

Similar to the student who avoids supervision is the student who does not think of consulting the supervisor. This student, when allocated a new piece of work, immediately becomes involved without seeking any discussion as to the best approach. The supervisor, attempting to encourage the student to reflect on the issues before beginning the work, is firmly resisted and confrontation is only avoided by allowing the student 'his/her head'. Such unresponsiveness to supervision might indicate that there are problems in the student's ability to learn from others and raises doubts about the progress which the student is capable of making. Where this is a clear pattern in a student's work it must be challenged, although the student's defensiveness might impede the supervisor's own ability to offer help. For example:

> M found it difficult to seek or accept help, information or advice from her supervisor. Capable in many areas of practice, she was insistent on doing things her way. It was leading to the danger of impoverishing her work, and when this was pointed out, anxiety about dependence and some previously unspoken resentments emerged. While independence continued to characterise her style, it was not the same degree and there was evidence of her taking in alternative perspectives from her supervisor and other staff.

The one-method student

Students at an early stage in their learning and not having a range of interventive methods at their disposal may become over-dependent on a method of work which is too limited for the range of problems that are faced in the agency. It may be that a student considers that particular method to be effective, having developed some skill in using it. The danger arises if the student considers that no help can be offered to a particular client because the problem would not be amenable to this particular favoured method. When this situation arises, the supervisor will need to encourage the student to consider the value of either a larger range of interventive methods or adopting a more eclectic approach to helping, combining a variety of understandings and techniques into a treatment plan rather than relying exclusively on one method. For example:

> A, a promising student with some experience of behavioural casework, but new to his Social Services placement, was allocated the case of a single parent who was finding it very difficult to cope with her two year-old child. After one visit, A suggested that the case be closed as the client was not responsive to the behavioural approach he had proposed. Following discussion in supervision and a further visit to the client, A referred the client to the playgroup and child-minder organiser who was able to arrange periods of alternative care for the child to give the client the respite that she desperately needed.

Avoiding involvement

All learning experiences involve students in feeling as well as thinking. Students who lack confidence in their ability to form relationships which involve the management of feelings may place great emphasis on the analysis of situations and tend to be resistant about involving themselves with the inter-personal relationship aspects of client problems, even where there might be clear evidence of a need for this. In this situation the supervisor will need not only to identify the difficulty, but also help the student understand the response required and gradually enable confidence to develop. For example:

> Although a competent student in many respects, D's practice was characterised by a lack of involvement with the feelings of clients, which impeded his overcoming problems when this was a component. Initially, when it was pointed out, it led to denial, anxiety and rather defensive rejection. However, with some firmness and support, it was overcome sufficiently for progress to be made and for the placement to succeed. This will probably be a feature of D's future work, particularly at the beginning of any new employment.

Over-identification

Towle suggests that 'students who invest themselves deeply out of a strong feeling for troubled people, are prone to let the client engulf them'. Furthermore, such 'empathy may cause the worker to permit the client to project his values and his problematic concerns upon the worker to an extent that the worker is helpless, because he feels like the client rather than himself'. Engulfed in the problems, the student is unable to begin objectively to analyse and assess the situation. However, once these students are helped to regulate their own feelings and needs, they often develop into very sensitive workers. For example:

> W combined both a very strong identification with the agency and his supervisor, and problems in learning. In some respects it was felt that the identification was a defence against having to examine weaknesses in his work. His learning was very slow. With help he began to show more independence, responsibility for his own ideas, and to show a quicker pace in learning.

The over-assertive student

Over-assertive students are often more difficult to help, as their own needs and opinions make it difficult for them to identify with people. Similarly, their ability to be open to learning must be seriously questioned. They should be confronted with those needs of clients that are being neglected and the difficulties created by their own need always to be in control. For example:

> J's over-assertive and even aggressive manner began to affect staff in the agency. She showed little awareness towards the problem and when confronted became distressed and had to take time out from the placement. Her manner was masking considerable insecurity and anxiety about her abilities. With counselling help she was able to resume the placement and complete it successfully.

Past experiences

Sometimes the demands of the placement situation can revive painful experiences for students. What is important is the extent to which the individual is accessible to experiences and relationships which correct the past. However, at the time of involvement with the case, the student may be confused, defensive and hostile about his or her feelings towards the client. The supervisor will need to face the student with the needs of the client which are not being met and encourage the student to develop insight into the relationship between the particular problem and the student's own needs. The insight that is gained should be used to deal with the current problem rather than to focus on the past personal experiences of the student. For example:

> When P began work with a family which featured an aggressive, authoritarian father, it provoked a considerable lengthy period of distress, which impeded her performance generally in the placement. It emerged that the work reactivated similar experiences from within P's own family. With support, and withdrawal from the particular case, the problem was overcome sufficiently for this otherwise very capable student to complete the placement successfully.

Personal difficulties which interfere with learning

Occasionally a student will experience personal difficulties beyond their control which interrupt the placement, either by causing a student to take time away from the placement, or result in emotional upset which prevents learning from taking place. In either situation, the tutor should be consulted. In many cases the student will still be able to achieve the goals of the placement. For example:

> B, a rather anxious and unconfident student, had his difficulties compounded by the loss of a close relative prior to the placement. It resulted in anxiety and depression and the need both for medical treatment and the support of the student counsellor. Although he failed the placement, the problems were eventually overcome and a further placement completed successfully.

The supervisor should avoid the temptation to 'casework' the student, by offering a therapeutic or counselling relationship, even if this is needed by the student. Where personal material is spontaneously brought into the supervisory relationship, it is very important that the supervisor makes no attempt to block it. A sympathetic ear should be offered and acceptance of the communication as evidence that the student was correct to confide, and as an indication to the supervisor of a willingness by the student to take responsibility for his/her own feelings. Taking care not to infer rejection of the material shared, the supervisor should nonetheless relate it only to the circumstances of the case at hand. Where it is clear that the experiences with which the student is coping are dysfunctional to work in a placement, the supervisor, in conjunction with the tutor, should encourage the student to seek therapeutic help, possibly from the student counselling service. On the rare occasions when a student's difficulties are having an adverse effect on their relationships in the agency or in work with clients, then a supervisor may insist on a student taking time out from the placement until sufficiently recovered to function again.

Where a contract has been based on erroneous information

We present here an example of how a supervisor might approach such a situation:

The student is on his second placement of a two-year CQSW course. Pre-placement discussions have taken place, and a clear and detailed contract has been negotiated and agreed to by all the parties involved. The student had fieldwork experience prior to the course and his first placement was in a hospital setting in which the supervisor indicated that the student was keen to learn and was of average potential.

The student feels that as a result of his experience to date, he has acquired some basic practice skills and reached a state of being able to make sound assessments. In the present placement he and his supervisor have agreed to concentrate on developing an appropriate interventive strategy and to build up confidence in at least one or two methods of working, particularly behaviour modification. A comment in the previous supervisor's report suggests that the student has a tendency to respond initially with defensiveness to feedback which includes criticism.

After three supervision sessions the supervisor is beginning to have doubts about whether the student can in fact organise information sufficiently well to arrive at appropriate assessments. In their sessions together a pattern is emerging in which the student is presenting copious information, both verbally and written, but then waiting expectantly for the supervisor to make sense of it. In their last session, when the supervisor asked for an analysis of the situation, the student was clearly floundering and seemed not to understand what the supervisor was expecting. The supervisor is now questioning whether the student has in fact acquired the necessary skill in assessment, and re-appraises the appropriateness of the learning goals of developing interventive skills for this placement.

Here are some points for consideration:

1. Has the supervisor clearly explained what is required by an analysis of the information?
2. If this has not already been done, the supervisor might test his or her doubts by asking for a written analysis for the next supervision session.
3. Although the previous supervisor's comments might have been made in good faith, that person's assessment of the student's stage of development could have been mistaken.
4. The student should be given critical feedback as soon as possible.
5. The supervisor needs to recognise the validity of the student's need to feel confident that he has a range of skills in his repertoire, but this work may not be able to proceed if it is not on the basis of abilities in assessment.
6. The possibility of renegotiating the learning tasks for the placement needs to be considered.
7. The student needs to be able not only to analyse information but to reorganise it in varied ways appropriate to the different kinds of situation.

Failing a student

Probably the most difficult situation for a practice teacher occurs when it becomes apparent that a student may have more than ordinary difficulties in learning and that the student may eventually be considered ineducable for social work. An ineducable student is one who has not been able to learn sufficiently to meet the required standard for the course and is therefore considered unsuitable for social work at that time. Recognising such a student is a serious dilemma for tutors and supervisors.

It is an understandable desire on the part of tutors and supervisors to want their students to be successful, and there may be resistance to recognising serious learning difficulties. On the other hand, they also want to help students to learn and believe that identifying difficulties and intervening early on is likely to be more helpful to a student. Certainly, supervisors should begin to work on the assumption that their student is educable for social work, until it is persistently proven that this is in doubt. Students have been selected to succeed on their social work course, but the selection process is not infallible, and on occasions there will be students who fail.

Serious problems which, if they persist, could lead to failure seem to manifest themselves in one of three broad areas of concern (Towle, 1954):

1. *Lack of motivation.* Here the student is insufficiently concerned to help clients, and their work will be marked by consistent lack of interest. The student is not affected by setbacks in cases and seems to have little at stake in their work.
2. *Excessive anxiety.* Here the student reacts to work situations with exceptional anxiety and stress, which remains unmodified over time. In such cases students may themselves conclude that they are unsuited to the work.
3. *Minimal learning.* Here the student shows compulsive repetition of unhelpful responses to clients, despite intellectual awareness of the problem and efforts to change, for example, is continually over-controlling or rejecting in behaviour to clients.

The ineducable learner

We have found it helpful to draw on the ideas of Charlotte Towle for criteria which tend to be present when the student

is ineducable. These students tend to remain in the beginning stages of learning:
1. In their dependence on supervision.
2. In their resistance to change, either by hostility towards the pressure which compels change or by submission to learning rather than participation in learning.
3. In their inability to relate the facts they are learning to the needs and demands of the situation.
4. The general or diffuse confusion of the early learning period extends and deepens, the confusion being reflected in several areas of work rather than being focalised on a particular problem.

The educable student

On the other hand, while the educable student may also suffer discomfort or become disturbed when their learning is obstructed:
1. Breakdown in competence is focalised and kept within limits. It does not extend generally over many aspects of their work. Nor does the student place responsibility for his or her difficulties elsewhere, either on the supervisor or their clients.
2. The student takes responsibility for dealing with the problem and strives to overcome it.
3. The student takes responsibility for seeking help.
4. The student is concerned for the client and does not take out their discomfort on clients, by either becoming neglectful or hostile as their own needs are unmet.
Furthermore, the educable student is able to make the most of supervision by:
1. Being able to take help without becoming overdependent or entering into conflict.
2. Being able to make productive use of the help offered.
3. Being receptive and not hypersensitive to criticism.
4. Being motivated to resolve the difficulty.
The educable student might not bring to social work the most appropriate motivation for the work, but has the capacity for change. Motivation falls into two general groupings: self-

centred aims and service aims. For the educable student the service aims will come to outweigh the self-centred aims.

Conclusion

Practice teachers who believe that their student has difficulty in learning, whether or not the student recognises it, need to avoid two possible unhelpful reactions:
1. Over-reaction, thus creating a further problem where there wasn't one.
2. Backing-off and failing to resolve the matter in their own minds, leaving themselves with misgivings, or leaving it to the next supervisor to discover and deal with.

When a difficulty is suspected, the supervisor must first ascertain whether the student knows clearly what is expected of them and secondly, question whether the student has been taught the necessary knowledge and skills prior to being expected to practice them. What might appear to be a symptom of some learning difficulty may simply require expectations to be clearly spelt out or the provision of some teaching input. With respect to any problem analysis, it is usually wiser to focus, in the first instance at least, on the role rather than the person. It is not always a simple matter to define the nature of a problem, particularly where the onus is on the supervisor to bring the apparent effects of it to the attention of the student. The process of helping a student to recognise that such a difficulty exists can cause anxiety and can sometimes be a painful experience for both student and supervisor, but nonetheless it is one which must be faced in the interests of the student, the agency and the client.

9

Evaluation, Assessment and Report Writing

While the main purpose of a placement is to provide the student with the opportunity to learn how to practise social work, it is necessary for the student's performance to be evaluated in order to check that an adequate standard is being reached.

Throughout a placement it should be the normal practice for supervisors to give their students regular feedback on how they are doing in the work they are undertaking. This process is commonly called evaluation. Periodically, perhaps at the request of the course staff, the supervisor will engage in a generalised feedback across the whole range of tasks undertaken by the student; this is usually referred to as assessment. Following the periodic assessment, a written report of the student's progress is submitted to the course staff.

Evaluation, or the feedback which is given to the student, can usefully be summed up as an explanation of the quality of certain aspects of the student's performance at specific points in time. It will take account of such matters as students' previous experience, their stage on the course, knowledge of the agency and the work at hand, the difficulty of the work, crises in the office, and personal pressures. Assessment, on the other hand, concerns the standard which all students on the course have to achieve. This standard may vary, depending on whether the placement is at the beginning of a course or towards the end. However, no allowance for special problems or circumstances can be made in mitigation when the assessment is made, although these factors will be taken into account subsequently by the course staff when they receive the report with the supervisor's recommendation. As the average performance of students on a course is inevitably the standard for that course, the performance of most students will not be of concern overall. Nonetheless, supervisors will be concerned to give them relevant feedback, which means that supervisors need clearly defined areas of performance on which to base their evaluations. Similarly, they need criteria on which to decide the relative quality of an individual student's overall performance compared to that of other students, and, less frequently, on whether a student should fail rather than pass the placement. In order to meet these responsibilities supervisors need:

1. An appropriate understanding of the authority invested in their role by the course staff.
2. A list of relevant areas of practice performance on which to give feedback to the student.
3. A range of reference points or criteria on which to draw, which will enable them to make a competent assessment of the student's standard of performance.

Furthermore, they must be able to communicate that evaluation and assessment to the course examiners in a form which comprehensively covers all areas of practice performance and provides sufficient evidence to support their opinions. It is to those ends that this chapter is devoted.

Problem

Len is a second-year student in his main and final placement. His supervisor begins to have misgivings about the quality of Len's performance with clients and is concerned about the slow progress in his learning. In her opinion Len appears to bring little reflection on his work to the supervision sessions and applies little of their discussions in the direct work with his clients. Two-thirds of the way through the placement the supervisor says that if Len's performance does not improve, he is at risk of failing the placement. Len is upset and critical of the supervisor, for allegedly not giving feedback on this degree of seriousness earlier and does not agree with it anyway. By the end of the placement the supervisor recommends that Len fails the placement. Len disagrees, feeling not only that the assessment is invalid, but that he has been treated unfairly, and appeals to the course examiners against the decision. The tutor, who has been involved throughout, is clear that Len's performance is poor, but because he is inexperienced in the role, the tutor is uncertain whether it is sufficiently poor to fail. The course's examiners' committee refers the matter to the external examiner, along with the placement report and a written appeal, with supporting case papers, from the student. The external examiner decides that while Len's performance is marginal, he has done enough to pass the placement. This view is accepted by the examiners' committee.

Question

Was this an appropriate way for the course examiners to deal with the matter? We think not. Unlike the academic work, where external examiners have access to exactly the same performance material as the original examiners, evidence of practice is even further removed from them than it is for tutors. For this reason it is not appropriate for anyone to attempt to re-mark practice in the way described. An individual or panel considering an appeal should limit the re-appraisal to the following issues:
1. Did the placement appear, on the face of it, to have been competently administered by the supervisor?
2. Was the assessment based on relevant factors, e.g. knowledge and skills?
3. Was the evidence offered to support opinions?
4. Was that evidence related to reasonable limits of attainment?
5. Were valid measures used as criteria for assessment?
As those conditions were met in the example, the assessment was a competent one and the supervisor's judgement should have been supported. The possibility of an injustice against the student would have been safeguarded by the offer of a further opportunity to complete a placement successfully.

The organisational context of evaluation and assessment

The relationship between the practice teacher and the tutor is appropriately regarded as a collaborative partnership to serve the learning interests of the student. However, this view alone of the relationship may not reveal the important elements in it, particularly those which are crucial to the supervisor's role in the assessment function. In our view it is only from a proper understanding of the responsibilities and the authority contained in their role that supervisors can act appropriately in giving feedback and setting the standard for the placement.

The body with the final responsibility for a student's education and training is the institution that has been authorised to provide the course; this institution is the ultimate authority. The groups designated to undertake the training within the institution vary, for example, both within universities and between them, and in other institutions of higher education such as polytechnics. However, they will all have in common:

1. A board of examiners, comprising staff competent to teach and examine in this subject area.
2. A procedure for appeal for students who disagree with the assessments made of them.
3. A body separate from the examiners, to which a student can appeal on the basis of procedure or personal circumstances.
4. An external examiner.

There are cases where appeals have been made to the University Visitor and to the courts, and presumably appeals could be taken to the European Court of Human Rights. The point we wish to make is that social work students have rights as well as obligations, and that social work supervision exists in an institutional context, which should be clearly understood by students, supervisors and tutors.

It is the responsibility of course examiners to select supervisors for their students; these are usually social workers competent to conduct and supervise the practice placement on behalf of the examiners. To avoid the time-consuming business of establishing the unique, individual competence of each potential practice teacher, the examiners will normally identify criteria which in principle ought to establish the competence of the social worker. They normally require the person to:

1. be a social worker;
2. be qualified by training;
3. have at least two years' post-qualifying experience;
4. have undertaken a course of preparation for their new role;
5. have been endorsed as suitable by their agency.

(The Central Council for Education and Training in Social Work has recently laid down its own, similar criteria for practice teachers, and has placed time limits within which social work courses must meet the requirements.)

When supervisors have met these criteria it should be assumed, unless demonstrated to the contrary, that their supervision and their assessment decisions will be competent. However, it is clear that the authority of supervisors stems from the course's examiners, and there is a viewpoint that it is the tutor, as an examiner, who should make the recommendation. This is not an unimportant issue, because not only do our later discussions depend on a resolution of these conflicting claims, but it may be an important reason why supervisors appear to be indecisive in assessing their students or indeed failing them, (Brandon & Davies, 1979; Morrell, 1980). On occasions when supervisors have made a recommendation that a student fail a placement, they feel that they are required to justify this decision, instead of the onus being on the student to justify his or her work.

If we accept that it is the examiners who take the responsibility for the final decision, who then should make the recommendation? More importantly, what is the basis for a competent decision on the recommendation that is made? It is difficult to see how the tutor can do this job. Only the supervisor has the detailed knowledge of the student's work. The tutor is necessarily dependent on that information, and even then is making the decision at secondhand. It seems clear to us that if the supervisor has made the recommendation on the criteria described earlier and has come to the decision in good faith, i.e. without evidence of malice towards the student, then the recommendation is competent and should be accepted. In retrospect, the decision may turn out to have been a mistaken one, but this possibility should be allowed for by appropriate safeguards for the student, such as the opportunity to undertake a further placement. The proper authority of supervisors should not be undermined by the removal from them of the responsibility for the recommendation.

The tutor does have an important contribution to make to this process. Not only should the supervisor consult the tutor, among others, on the issue of standards, but if the issue of failing arises, the tutor has a crucial role. Unlike the supervisor, tutors with even relatively brief experience in the role will have observed the work of a large range of students. Thus they will be in a position to locate an individual student's performance within the range of performances of a large number of fellow students. As we pointed out earlier, there is no abstract, adequate standard of performance among social work students; the student group as a whole is the standard for entrants to the profession at any point in time. If a student is failing, then it would be expected that that student's performance falls below the average performance of the student body as a whole. The validity of a supervisor's judgement in a particular instance will depend in part on their willingness to accept guidance from the tutor on that particular aspect of the assessment. Thus a tutor's contribution should be limited to deciding whether the student's performance falls below the average for the group and so places the individual at risk of failing.

Tutor and supervisor have different but complementary responsibilities to the social work profession. Tutors in their role as teachers have a responsibility to educate their students for social work and to prepare them to make the best use of the training aspect of the course. Supervisors have the responsibility of providing students with guided opportunities to apply that understanding on behalf of clients. Both tutor and supervisor need to ensure that the education and training of any student has reached an adequate standard when it is expressed in action. They reflect, however, quite different constituencies. The supervisor represents the working profession and the standards of acceptable practice to that group. The tutor represents the concern to replenish the profession regularly with dependable entrants. The former represents concern for absolute standards of acceptability at the point of completion; the latter ensures that a student is considered fairly in the context of reasonable expectations of all the students in training. It is in the tension between these two aspects that the academic and practice elements are constantly considered within social work education and training.

The basis for a competent assessment

If a practice teacher is to conduct the supervision of the student's work competently, then it is clear that the grounds upon which evaluation is to be based must be known to both beforehand. Otherwise, feedback cannot be given concurrently as the placement develops. Assessment, whether at the interim or final stage of the placement, is an accumulation of continuous feedback and periodic informal 'assessments': hence the 'golden rule' that students should learn nothing new of significance at the assessment stage. If they do, it indicates a failing on the part of a supervisor, especially where the additional evaluations are negative. Nonetheless, the requirements of assessment are absolute, and however 'unfair' the information, it should be included. Otherwise, the assessment is dishonest, and if the material is significant, it may also be incompetent. The priority of an assessment report is neither to protect the welfare of a student nor the image of a practice teacher, but the future recipients of a social work service.

Let us assume that the placement has been executed competently and the supervisor is preparing for the final assessment stage with the student. What factors should the supervisor take into account in deciding whether the quality of the student's performance overall has met the appropriate standard for the course? This is not a difficult task in the great majority of instances, where failing is not an issue, and so it is probably useful to scrutinise the validity of the following discussion as though it were in respect of performance which is marginal. The following process and content factors are offered as a guide. It will be assumed that the supervisor is competently qualified and prepared for the role and has a clear understanding of the organisational context of his or her responsibilities.

A framework of areas of practice performance

All social work courses identify areas or aspects of their students' practice on which they require their supervisors to focus for the purposes of assessment. Some courses spell out these areas in more detail than others, but even where checklists or gradings are used, supervisors are usually asked to provide descriptive evaluation and illustration of the work. A performance framework defines the boundaries of what will be included for assessment. These performance areas do not undermine the fact that the meaning and quality of a student's performance has to be arrived at through the individual judgement of a supervisor, but they do determine the grounds on which that judgement will be made. They form a significant element in the contract of expectations between the student, the supervisor and the course through the role of the tutor, and will have provided the base from which a more individualised learning contract is made for that particular placement.

The course run by the School of Social Work at the University of Leicester has specified its framework of performance in some detail, for community work, residential social work and fieldwork (agency) placements (Leicester University School of Social Work, 1982; Curnock and Prins, 1982). For example, in respect of its agency placements it has identified twenty-four distinct aspects of performance, covering five broad areas on which the student's performance is assessed. These broad areas cover:
1. the student as a learner, including use of supervision;
2. the availability and application of relevant knowledge;
3. the ability to work within the agency;
4. activity with clients and others;
5. attitudes and values expressed in the work.

The Leicester course argues that performance extends beyond the student's activities directly or indirectly with clients. To make the best use of the placement, the student must be able to engage and use knowledge effectively and use a teaching/learning relationship productively. However, not all aspects are equally important, and some are more crucial than others in assessing performance. For example, it may be possible to make an allowance for some failure to work co-operatively with other workers in an agency if other aspects are positive, but if a student consistently fails to be able to make acceptable initial contacts with clients, then this would certainly lead to failing, as it would make most of the other aspects irrelevant. One consideration that course examiners will have in mind, then, when considering the competence of a supervisor's assessment, is whether it is based on the relevant grounds. Where a course provides few grounds or imprecise ones, there is a greater onus on the supervisor to formulate the basis of the assessment. Where a course provides grounds in more detail, it will expect that a comprehensive assessment will, at the minimum, cover them all. They will leave it to a supervisor to decide whether it is necessary to go beyond them, by including additional aspects of performance.

A range of indicators of positive and negative performance

All practice teachers have in mind a range of ideas about what constitutes good and bad social work practice. At the very least, they know both types when they see them and in respect of many aspects of performance they probably have very clear ideas. Asked out of the blue, however, they would probably have some difficulty in giving a comprehensive account of what they mean. On some aspects they might continue to be uncertain. In relation to the performance areas on which a course requires comment, unless it provides indicators, the supervisors would in practice search their own experience for such guidelines. Then the challenge would be in identifying the degree to which the student's performance was positive or negative. The University of Leicester School of Social Work provides comprehensive positive and negative indicators of performance in respect of its practice placements. In respect of a student's performance, it believes that it has a responsibility to offer to students and practice teachers an authoritative view of the basis on which a judgement should be taken. Supervisors are not obliged to use the indicators in their evaluations and assessments of students, but where they are in doubt they are provided with an opportunity to obtain the School's opinion as a first point of reference.

In social work, students' performance has traditionally been judged on how they go about their work – their inputs, if you like, rather than on the effectiveness or outcome of their work. This is a sound practice on the whole, because an unsuccessful outcome is not evidence that the input was inappropriate or that the work was without effort and commitment. However, the Leicester School of Social Work believes there is, on the basis of theory and from experience, an increasingly plausible relationship between input and outcome. With safeguards, outcome could offer evidence in relation to the quality of the input. For example, a positive outcome in a case would call into doubt a negative view of an input. Similarly, where in the opinion of a supervisor the original input has been poor, one would expect it to be supported by a less-than-positive outcome or indeed an actively negative one. An illustration of the use of indicators from the *Practice Guide* of the Leicester University School of Social Work, is offered below (Curnock and Prins, p. 518):

Skill in exploration of facts and feelings relevant to the client's problems
(input)

Student shows respect for the validity of the clients' own understanding of their situations; understands that facts about experience must be appreciated in the context of the feelings associated with them; values the needs of clients to explore their situations in order to be able to make choices about actions; is

Student is too passive or only able to respond to communicative clients; is too directive or controlling; blocks relatively mild feelings through anxiety; is unable to distinguish between prying into and exploring people's problems; insensitive to obvious indications of distress or stress; unable to 'listen' to able to respond to feelings towards him including negative ones; he can discuss his own feelings about work with particular clients.

what the client is saying; inept in helping the client to structure his understanding of problems in order to enhance control of them.

(outcome)

Most clients are able to talk to the student about their difficulties; strong feelings are accepted (not without difficulty necessarily) and the student is developing skills in 'reaching out' to clients where appropriate; indications that some clients are sustained by the student's efforts; evidence of client's enhanced motivation to solve problems.

Work tends to be vague and undirected; not much 'movement' in cases or indications of initiative on the student's part; evidence of dissatisfied clients; little evidence of knowledge gained being related to work goals; avoiding some clients where strong feelings are a feature.

A developmental performance learning model in which to locate the standard

It is in the nature of complex learning that it usually involves progression: from the beginning stage of initial acquaintance, to a final stage of relative competence. The speed of acquisition of knowledge and skills will depend in part on the range and complexity of the elements to be accomplished, and on the aptitudes of the learner. With respect to learning in social work practice, it has been suggested that the process follows identifiable and predictable stages; furthermore, that the performance of average students as they progress chronologically through the course can be identified as lying within certain stages. If these claims are correct, they could prove to be helpful in providing a further perspective for the supervisor both in understanding the nature of a student's overall performance at any stage in a placement, and as possible clues to setting appropriate standards. In respect of social work students such a model is offered by Bertha Reynolds (1965). Reynolds identifies the stages of learning and students' responses as follows:

1. *Acute self-consciousness.* Students frequently experience this during first placements and the early phases of all placements, but it should only be a temporary phase and any paralysis should be short-lived.
2. *Sink or swim adaptation (trial and error).* This stage may be relatively long and students characteristically 'talk better than they do'.
3. *Understanding the situation without the power to control one's activity in it.* This is a characteristic feature of much social work practice, but it is often particularly acute in professional training; many social workers display an intellectual grasp of situations but are unable to translate this into action.
4. *Relative mastery in understanding and controlling one's activity.* This stage epitomises good professional practice, when knowledge and skills become an internalised part of the student's repertoire.

The Leicester University School of Social Work has experimented with this model in setting its assessment standards. A lower standard was set for a first placement (stage 2 primarily, with some aspects in stage 3) and a higher standard (stage 3, with some elements in stage 4) for a later, final or main placement. It seems unlikely that such a model can be used with precision to set a standard for assessing performance, but it does provide a useful perspective for the practice teacher.

A procedure to safeguard the competence of the assessment, and the rights of the student

The procedure should consist of a sequence of steps which act as a balance or corrective against the possibility of idiosyncratic errors on the part of the practice teacher. Initial steps would include obtaining the opinion of other colleagues who have been involved with the student during the period of placement. It would also involve consulting with and testing out the evaluation with the supervisor's line manager. Where serious criticism of the student's work is involved, it would require discussion with the tutor and evidence to support the negative views. Where failing was being considered, the student would be advised of the grounds for it and the procedures for appeal.

The compilation of a report

The report should not only clearly indicate the standard which the supervisor believes has been reached by the student, but also make the reasoning and justification of the judgement accessible to the student and to other relevant people, such as examiners. The latter are required to confirm that the grounds on which the assessment has been made are relevant, and the judgement reasonable and understandable at face value. This requires that the report should give a sufficiently detailed description of the performance of the student's work in the placement, with illustration and evidence to support the opinions given.

The supervisor's competence

It is an inescapable fact that all the other assessment criteria can only be brought to bear through the judgement of the supervisor. Supervisors who feel nervous of that fact should merely reflect that there is no alternative; there is nobody better placed to assume the responsibility. All professions are inevitably dependent on their own members for the provision of the education and training necessary to replenish their numbers; in the nature of things they not only set the standard, they are the standard. Choosing practice teachers is the method of setting the standard for controlling entry to the occupation. Supervisors are able to take into account the standard that was set in their own training; the standard they achieved themselves as students; the standards of their fellow students; the standards of new colleagues to social work; and the standards achieved by students supervised by other colleagues. If supervisors can take confidence from that understanding, follow the procedures suggested above and base their judgement on appropriate grounds, then they may be confident that they will always make a competent, even if not always correct, judgement about the performance of a student. A mistaken judgement is to be regretted, but decisions have to be faced. As long as it is competent and made in good faith, it should be possible to bear the burden of responsibility. Course examiners should support such a decision and see it as a separate issue, for them alone, with regard to what they do subsequently in respect of a student who has failed a placement.

Report writing

Little is known about supervisor's attitudes to preparing and writing their placement reports on students. However, after a placement is completed, it is the only tangible evidence left to the course staff of the nature and quality of the placement and of the performance of the student.

Most tutors and practice teachers would probably recognise both very good and very bad reports when they saw them. What is perhaps more difficult for the individual supervisor is to decide in advance:

1. the kind of information that should be included in a comprehensive report; and
2. the types of knowledge that are required in order to convey competently the nature of the student's performance.

Following a survey and analysis of a large number of supervisors' reports, we believe we have identified the important elements in both the *form* and *content* of a comprehensive and competent supervisor's report. These elements will be described and illustrated from typical reports (Jones, 1981).

All placement reports can be divided into two aspects, which we define as *form* and *content*. The aspects which make up the *form* of a report are the kinds of *information* which are necessary for a comprehensive report in a particular type of placement, e.g. fieldwork, residential care, community work. The *content* aspects are the various kinds of *knowledge* which are intrinsic to the completion of any practice report, irrespective of the form of the report.

The following are the items which should make up the form of the report for a placement in a fieldwork agency:

1. An indication of the degree of difficulty of the work that has been undertaken by the student, as compared with the usual range of work in the agency.
2. A list of the cases, tasks or work undertaken, so that a picture is provided of the overall workload of the student during the placement.
3. Summaries of a sample of the work listed, either provided by the student or the supervisor. This is optional, depending on whether supervisors prefer to write their own account of the work undertaken by the student, which would then be incorporated within the body of the report as a whole. Some supervisors prefer their students to write the case summaries and then to refer to them appropriately throughout the body of their own report.
4. The performance areas which the course stipulates are to be the framework within which the student's placement must be evaluated – for example, the student's ability to form relationships with clients, or their ability to form effective working relationships with colleagues in the agency.
5. A clear indication of the overall standard of the student's practice that has been reached in the placement, at least indicating whether the work has reached an acceptable standard.

It is our contention that if all these elements are contained in the placement report, then it will form the basis of a comprehensive account of a student's performance.

It is up to the supervisor to decide how the report will be written within this format. However, it appears from reports which we have studied that whatever the form of the report, supervisors typically *describe* the performance of their student's work, offer *illustrations*, provide *evidence* for their own views, *explain* the performance and, finally, come to *judgements* about the standard which the student has achieved in each separate aspect which makes up their total performance. We believe that these are the types of knowledge which lay the basis for a comprehensive assessment report, as long as they are integrated appropriately within the style of the individual supervisor.

Below is a list of the constituents of content. We explain

these in rather more detail and present examples of their usage from actual teachers' reports:

Description (what the student has done). The report should describe what has been undertaken within each of the performance aspects, for example skill in exploration of facts and feelings. The extent of description can vary with the presence or absence of case studies or case summaries. It sometimes conveys what has changed over time, which can give it the appearance, and an element, of analysis. It can be seen as laying the ground for the next two stages, of evaluation (analysis) and assessment (synthesis), and will often contain the suggestion of a strength or a problem.
Example (referring to goal-setting and focused work): 'This has featured as an important area, much of it connected to the enforced limits of the end of the placement'.

Illustration. This is an example from the work undertaken, which exemplifies or makes something concrete, in order to bring a narrative to 'life' or to link it firmly to the case studies. Example: 'aspects of [student's] previous training in science and engineering have been useful to him, e.g. [references to two cases] . . . he was able to record their response to a behaviour modification programme in graph form'.

Evidence. This is more than a single illustration, in order to support a more weighty valuation of either a positive or negative indication of performance.
Example: 'T uses his relationship with clients to enable them to express their feelings without fear of rejection and he copes well with the wide range of emotions expressed by clients [then follow four case examples of different facets of managing relationships well] – aggression, fear and guilt, unresponsiveness, passivity and negativeness, and denial.'

Evaluation (analysis). This concerns the way in which the student has performed. It is an educational analysis of a particular performance aspect. It takes the form of a volume of comments, defining, explaining, weighing, interpreting or placing in context the nature of the performance. Its aim is to explain to the student and to the course the meaning and quality of the performance as perceived by the supervisor. Example: 'In weekly supervision he has shown a good knowledge of human behaviour in interaction with the environment and in reaction to stress. Whenever he has felt his existing knowledge is inadequate he has always sought information in discussion with colleagues, or read around the subject' [followed by two illustrations from cases, one on school refusal and the other on family therapy].

Assessment (synthesis). This concerns how the student has done. It is an indication of the quality of achievement reached in relation to each aspect of performance. It is a statement of synthesis and demands that no allowance is made for any factors which may have influenced the standard reached. It refers to achievement, not to the degree of effort or striving. Example: 'He has shown considerable skill in setting realistic goals and being aware of the differences involved in this kind of work from long-term intensive casework'.

The following is an example of a statement which combines description, evaluation and assessment:

> A began to write reports diffidently, with an understandable reluctance to record his professional opinion for the court [description]. When he established the level of persuasion and judgement which the court would take [evaluation], he wrote well argued, concise and helpful reports [assessment].

Then follow four pieces of evidence illustrating aspects of these skills. The final comment is: 'there is no doubt that one of A's great values to the agency is his communication skill on paper' [assessment].

10

Endings

In earlier chapters we have emphasised the need for careful thought and planning in preparing for practice teaching. Our aim here is to encourage the practice teacher to consider the implications of the placement ending and to plan for this, so as to minimise for all parties concerned the disruptive effects of change. We will be considering some of the theoretical concepts of change and loss that seem to be relevant, and will look at the significance of the end of the placement for those involved. In Chapter 3 we identified the contract as the cornerstone of the placement because it provides an 'agenda'. In this chapter, we look at the notion of there being 'business' that has to be properly completed if the contract is to be met by the end of the placement. Rituals are widely used in our society to dramatise change, and in this final chapter we consider the value of this concept as a way of publicly dealing with the separation, so that all parties feel the contract has been satisfactorily concluded.

Thus we suggest that in order to bring a placement to a satisfactory, if not successful, conclusion, one important aim for the student is not to carry away from the placement thoughts and feelings that could have been dealt with during the placement. We will be looking at the experience of ending the placement from the perspective of all the participants: student, supervisor, tutor and team colleagues. There are four main tasks to be completed:
1. bringing the work to a proper completion;
2. dealing with feelings: here we refer to ideas of loss and change;
3. working through any 'unfinished business';
4. a ritualised ending to the placement through ceremony.

144

Significance of the ending of the placement for all of the participants

Change usually means that a familiar pattern of relationships is disrupted. Peter Marris (1974) suggests that 'whenever people are confronted by change, they need the opportunity to react, to articulate their ambivalent feelings and work out their own defence of it'. At the end of a placement there are many feelings around to which the supervisor needs to be sensitive. Particularly if this has been a first placement for either, it is an important ending for both the supervisor and the student. For professional colleagues, too, the end of the student's placement will have significance, even if they have seen many students come and go.

The student

Social work students are in a particularly difficult situation. Maturity is thought to be a desirable personal attribute and an important criterion in selecting students to undertake social work training. However, the people who meet this criterion are likely to be competent people who have been in paid employment and who now find themselves back in a dependent student role. (The particular difficulties of the adult learner have been discussed in more detail in Chapter 8.) In addition, the social work student is then expected to progress through a series of transitions during the course, alternating between the academic environment and the practice placement. Each change will cause anxiety of varying degrees to the student.

At the end of each practice placement, students will have a number of things to deal with:

Terminating work. Whatever the type of placement, the student will be bringing to a conclusion the tasks he or she has been involved in: by evaluating progress; making future plans; drawing together loose ends; and reminding people that they are leaving. They will be negotiating for work to be continued by someone else or they, and perhaps their clients too, may be facing the prospect that no future social work intervention will be offered. If interventions have been well planned and clear contracts have been made concerning the student's involvement, this will ease withdrawal. However, there will still be work for the student in helping clients understand and come to terms with feelings aroused by the social work involvement being terminated. The student, too, is faced with the loss of clients and the satisfaction that some of these relationships will have given.

Loss of role. With the end of the placement comes the loss of role, at least temporarily, as a social worker. This is the professional role that the student is striving for, and one of the purposes of the practice placement is to give students the opportunity to test themselves out in this role. Some students experience a loss of status in returning once again to the academic student role. For the final placement student there might be anxiety about future employment.

In most practice placements, the student will have been a member of a team. The amount of support offered by the team and the extent to which the student has become integrated will determine the degree of loss felt by the student for colleagues. Similarly, if the supervisory relationship has been satisfying and the student feels that the desired progress has been made, the student will experience a sense of loss at losing these learning opportunities.

Other pressures. There will be other pressures on the student as the placement draws to a close: for example practical problems of getting recording or report writing up to date, or anxiety as to what actually gets written in the assessment report. In Chapter 5 we stressed the importance of continual feedback and evaluation throughout the placement to ensure there are no 'surprises' for the student when it comes to the assessment. The student will nevertheless feel concerned until the actual content of the report is known.

The team

In most practice placement settings, team colleagues will
have made an important contribution to the student's
learning: individuals may have co-worked cases with the
student or shared work on projects, or the team may have
been asked to make a contribution to the assessment of the
student. To the team, particularly one well motivated to
receiving students on a regular basis, the student will often
have become a welcome and well integrated colleague. In
practical ways the team may miss the student's contribution to sharing the workload; in a more abstract way, it
may miss the contribution of a new person, perhaps
bringing a refreshing, stimulating perspective to team
discussions. As a personality, the student may have
brought a new dimension to the group dynamics. The
significance of the student's impact on an office may not be
felt until after the placement has ended, and occasionally a
student will become a 'legend' in an office, to be remembered and referred to as a positive or negative experience
in many subsequent discussions on student supervision.

In Chapter 2 on pre-placement planning, we emphasised that the student is on placement to the agency and
not to the supervisor, and suggested that prospective
supervisors would need to negotiate with colleagues
before committing themselves to taking a student. The
team will have been involved in discussions on how many
students they could support at any one time, the contribution of the team to the student's learning, and the
implications of the supervisor not being available to take a
normal share of the workload. The more the team has
been involved in the placement, however, the greater the
impact of the student's departure. The team collectively
will experience the loss and may collectively wish to
express this to the student.

The supervisor

The end of a practice placement can be a demanding time
for the supervisor.

Practical considerations. It is often the writing of the assessment report that dominates the supervisor's time and energies. However, there is also an appreciable amount of administrative work involved in ensuring that appropriate future action is taken on the work the student has been doing. In addition, there will usually be an end-of-placement visit by the tutor to organise and plan for.

Own feelings. Amidst the other demands, there is perhaps little time for supervisors to deal with their own feelings at the end of the placement. These might range from relief that the demands of having a student are over to a feeling of anti-climax. Overall, one would hope that there is a sense of achievement in having contributed to the learning and professional development of the student.

The supervisor not only loses the student as a person, someone in whom a great deal of time and energy has been invested, but also the opportunities for new learning which the exchange will have offered. In addition, the supervisor loses the status of being a student supervisor, someone who has been recognised as having the ability to teach a new practitioner the role and skills involved. Some supervisors miss the contact and relationship they may have enjoyed with the tutor and the educational establishment, particularly if the latter has offered additional support by way of supervisors' meetings.

Feelings of the student. The way in which the supervisor deals with the student's feelings at the end of the placement can provide a useful model for the student in terminating relationships with clients at the end of the placement. Indeed, some would argue that the student's relationships throughout the placement will be mirrored or reflected in what is going on in supervision and *vice versa* (Heap, 1975). Thus the investment made by the supervisor in the student will provide a model for the student's investment in clients. Supervisors need, therefore, to acknowledge the end of the placement and the loss of the student to themselves, the team and the agency in the fullest possible way, thereby allowing the student to express his or her own feelings.

Change and loss

It seems relevant at this point to examine the feelings of loss which might be experienced by the student at the end of a practice placement, in the light of a theoretical perspective. Marris identifies three types of change:
1. Substitutional or incremental changes. Examples of these would be a new job, new house, etc.
2. Change that represents loss – for example, bereavement, divorce, etc. ·
3. Change that represents growth. These changes do not threaten the integrity of what has already been learned. As Marris says, 'a growing person is confident enough to explore new experiences just because the basis of under-standing seems secure and the sense of continuity is still unbroken'.

If we think of the social work student in the context of a learning continuum, there are ultimate goals to be achieved which provide a meaningful structure to the process of transition. This seems to put the loss that potentially might be experienced by the student in a more positive light: each transition, although accompanied by varying degrees of stress, is a step closer to the ultimate goal. Because the imminent change can be anticipated, adjustment to the loss can be partly prospective, and by the final days of the placement, disengagement, emotionally as well as practi-cally, has begun to take place. Nevertheless, the transition will cause some stress for the student even if the loss is peripheral. The degree of loss felt will ultimately depend on the degree of emotional investment in the placement.

What the supervisor can do to help in the student's transition

The aim naturally at the end of the placement should be that all parties are left with the feeling that the contract has been satisfactorily concluded. At the very least the placement should be completed efficiently, and as far as possible there should not be any unfinished business which has not been discussed and given an opportunity to be worked through. The feelings of loss experienced by students should hopefully be dealt with within the placement, thus leaving them 'free' to move into the next stage of the course without having too many unresolved feelings from the placement to take away with them.

We have suggested that training relationships must be congruent with the work the learner is expected to do with those they are helping. Thus, if students have been expected to involve themselves with clients' feelings, then we must expect them to be able to discuss their own feelings about their work. This process is likely to deepen students' investment of feelings in the work and in the agency. When they leave they will need to be able to separate, emotionally as well as physically, from their work and the colleagues associated with it.

As students are to become workers who can recognise their own feelings and deal with them appropriately (as they will have helped clients to deal with theirs), then they should be helped not to form unhelpful defences against those feelings at the time they are leaving the placement. The placement has encouraged an investment of feelings, and students now need to be helped to withdraw them. They can do this by talking about their experiences with the people involved and to express the feelings they have about leaving them. The student may not be used to doing this and may need a clear indication that it is permissible and may also need help in doing so.

Assessment report

The assessment report is tangible evidence of the end of the placement, and we would suggest that having a copy of the final report to take away symbolises for the student that the business of the placement has been completed. Among other pressures at the end of the placement, supervisors might be tempted to feel that the final draft of the report can be left until after the student leaves. We would suggest, however, that this is bad practice, and that until the final report is typed and available to the student, there may still be 'unfinished business' between the student and supervisor which can leave the student feeling, at best, that residues from the placement have to be carried over into the next phase of the course, or, at worst, angry that the supervisor has possibly denied the student the right to challenge the report or aspects of it. The content of the report should be discussed and agreed upon as far as possible, and the student should be presented with a copy before leaving the placement. It is not satisfactory merely to discuss the content of the report with the student: there should be an opportunity to comment on the final draft. Similarly, it is not satisfactory if the student has to return to the placement to discuss the final draft, or it has to be sent on to the student for comments.

It is unlikely that any unfinished business can be dealt with until the report is completed. Once the report is concluded, students and supervisors have the opportunity to come out of their respective roles and, if they wish, to use the opportunity for an honest appraisal of the placement from both sides. This is an opportunity for supervisors to evaluate their own input into the placement and to assess their abilities as practice teachers. It is also time to review any lost learning opportunities.

Rituals

Rituals, or 'rites of passage' as Nicky Hart (1976) refers to them, are symbolic ways of marking change in status. They are common in our society: for example, the change of status that accompanies marriage is marked by ceremony; the traditional hymn sung at a school-leaving ceremony is a similar ritual, but marks the changing status of a group rather than an individual. At the end of a practice placement, a ceremony can be a dramatic way of saying that the business is finished and the student is free to move on with 'full public knowledge and approval'. Teams and agencies establish their own individual traditions, which become part of the office culture, to mark this transition and acknowledge the loss. For these reasons they are probably more important to students than colleagues might appreciate. It is a good idea for students to have something to take away with them, besides the placement report! This could be a card signed by all members of the team, a cartoon drawn by an artistically minded colleague, or a small gift, although this is less practicable if many students come and go. The traditional gift given to students when they left one particular social services area team was the 'Jargon Generator', illustrated in Figure 10.1. This was designed as an aid to aspiring social workers to ensure liberal use of jargon in their reports!

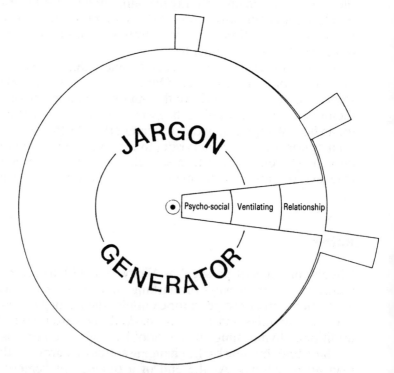

Figure 10.1 *Jargon generator*

Source: Compiled by Les Gallop, based on 'Puck's Primer' and illustrated in *Psycho Sources: a Psychology Resource Catalogue* (1972), edited by Evelyn Shapiro from the publishers of *Psychology Today* (USA).

In other placements, the student's leaving is marked by a farewell drink in the pub, students and supervisor going for a meal together or an office outing. One offce used students' leavings as an excuse to plan elaborate meals and picnics, which had a dual purpose of bonding team members. Rituals can be embarrassing, particularly for a student unaccustomed to being the centre of attention, so the supervisor and team, in planning to mark the end of the placement, will need to be sensitive to the feelings of the student and plan accordingly. It is not every student who would be able to cope with the 'passing out' ceremony we heard about in one office. At the farewell gathering the student was given three words to link together in one sentence: the words might be fashionable jargon in the office, words the student frequently used, or one might be the name of a renowned client. Once the student had made their sentence they were deemed to have 'graduated' from the placement.

References

Ainley, M. and Kingston, P. (1981) 'Live Supervision in a Probation Setting', *Social Work Education*, vol. 1, no. 1, August.

Barclay, P. (1982) *Social Workers: their Roles and Tasks*, London, Bedford Square Press.

Barker, D. L. and Allen, S. (eds) (1976) *Dependence and Exploration in Work and Marriage*, London, Longman.

Bartlett, H. M. (1970) *The Common Base of Social Work Practice*, New York, NASW.

Berne, E. (1964) *Games People Play*, Harmondsworth, Penguin.

Brandon, J. and Davies, M. (1979) 'The Limits of Competence in Social Work: the Assessment of Marginal Students in Social Work Education', *British Journal of Social Work*, vol. 9, no. 3.

Button, L. (1971) *Discovery and Experience: a New Approach to Training, Groupwork and Teaching*, London, Oxford University Press.

Caplan, G. (1961) *An Approach to Community Mental Health*, London, Tavistock.

Carpenter, J. and Deschrer, J. (1982) 'Using Role Plays in Teaching and Assessing Family Therapy Skills', *Social Work Education*, vol. 2, no. 11, Winter, pp. 12–17.

CCETSW (1983) Paper 21, *Teaching Social Work for a Multi-racial Society*, CCETSW.

Cheetham, J. (ed.) (1981) *Social and Community Work in a Multi-racial Society*, London, Harper & Row.

Cheetham, J. (ed.) (1982) *Social Work and Ethnicity*, London, Allen and Unwin.

Coates, K. and Silburn, R. (1973) *Poverty – the Forgotten Englishmen*, Harmondsworth, Penguin.

Curnock, K. and Prins, H. (1982) 'An Approach to Fieldwork Assessment', *British Journal of Social Work*, vol. 12, no. 5, pp. 507–32.

Davies, M. (1984) 'Training: What Do We Think of it Now?', *Social Work Today*, 24 January, pp. 12–17.

Davis, H. (1977) *Student Group Supervision*, Family Service Units.

Dominelli, L. (1979) 'The Challenge for Social Work Education', *Social Work Today*, vol. 10, no. 25.

Gallop, L. and Quinn, M. (1981) 'Slow, Slow, Quick Quick . . .', *Community Care*, no. 367, p. 12.

Germain, C. B. (1979) *Social Work Practice: People and Environments: an Ecological Perspective*, Columbia University Press.

Germain, C. B. and Gitterman, A. (1980) *The Life Model of Social Work Practice*, Columbia University Press.

Goldstein, H. (1973) *Social Work Practice: a Unitary Approach*, University of South Carolina Press.

Gullerad, E. N. (1977) 'Planning – Professional Educational Programmes for Ethnic Minority Students: Native American Examples', *Journal of Education for Social Work*, vol. 13, no. 1, pp. 68–75.

Hart, N. (1976) *When Marriage Ends*, London, Tavistock.

Hartnett, O. Boden, G. and Fuller, M. (1979) *Sex Role Stereotyping*, London, Tavistock.

Heap, E. (1975) 'The Supervisor as Reflector', *Social Work Today*, vol. 5, no. 22.

Howard, J. and Gooderham, P. (1975) 'Closed Circuit TV in Social Work Training', *Social Work Today*, vol. 6, no. 7.

Howe, D. (1979) 'Agency Function and Social Work Principles', *British Journal of Social Work*, vol. 9, no. 1, pp. 29–49.

Ivey, A. *et al.* (1968) 'Microcounselling and Attending Behaviour: an Approach to Prepracticum Counsellor Training', *Journal of Counselling Psychology*, monograph supplement, vol. 15, pp. 1–12.

Ivey, A. and Authier, J. (1975) *Microcounselling*, 2nd edn, Illinois, C. C. Thomas.

Johnson, T. (1972) *Professions and Power*, London, Macmillan.

Jones, A. (1981) *Monitoring the Quality of Fieldwork Reports*, University of Leicester School of Social Work.

Kingston, P. and Smith, D. (1983) 'Preparations for Live Consultation and Live Supervision When Working with a One-Way Screen', *Journal of Family Therapy*, no. 5, pp. 219–33.

Knowles, M. (1973) *The Adult Learner: a Neglected Species*, Gulf Publications.

Leicester University School of Social Work (1982) *Practice Guide*, 2nd edn.

Leicester University School of Social Work (1984) 'Non-Sexist Language in Social Work', unpublished paper by staff and students.

Leicester University School of Social Work (1984) 'Monitoring the quality of practice placements', unpublished paper.

Lewis, H. (1972) 'Developing a Program Responsive to New Knowledge and Values', in Mullen, E. J., Dumpson, J. R. and Associates (eds) *Evaluation of Social Intervention*, Jossey Bass.

Marris, P. (1974) *Loss and Change*, London, Routledge & Kegan Paul.

Mattinson, J. (1975) *The Reflection Process in Casework Supervision*, Institute of Marital Studies.

Meltzer, R. (1977) 'School and Agency Cooperation in Using Videotape in Social Work Education', *Journal of Education for Social Work*, vol. 13, no. 1, pp. 90–5.

Middleman, R. R. and Goldberg, G. (1974) *Social Service Delivery: a Structured Approach*, Columbia University Press.

Miller, C. and Swift, K. (1981) *The Handbook of Non-Sexist Writing for*

156 References

Workers, Editors and Speakers, London, Women's Press.

Miller, H. L. (1966) *Teaching and Learning in Adult Education*, New York, Macmillan.

Mitchell, J. and Oakley, A. (1976) *The Rights and Wrongs of Women*, Harmondsworth, Penguin.

Morrell, E. (1980) 'Student Assessment: Where Are We Now?', *British Journal of Social Work*, vol. 10, no. 4.

Parsloe, P. (1978) 'The Use of Contracts on a Social Work Course', in Stevenson, O. (ed.) *Trends in Social Work Education*, ATSWE/Alden Press.

Pettes, D. E. (1967) *Supervision in Social Work: a Method of Student Training and Staff Development*, London, Allen & Unwin.

Pincus, A. and Minahan, A. (1973) *Social Work Practice: Model and Method*, F. E. Peacock.

Prins, H. (undated) a talk to supervisors at the Leicester University School of Social Work.

Reid, W. J. and Epstein, L. (1972) *Task-centred Casework*, Columbia University Press.

Reid, W. J. and Epstein, L. (1977) *Task-centred Practice*, Columbia University Press.

Reynolds, B. (1965) *Learning and Teaching in the Practice of Social Work*, New York, Russell & Russell.

Rhim, B. C. (1976) 'The Use of Videotapes in Social Work Agencies', *Social Casework*, December, pp. 644–50.

Robinson, M. (1978) 'Contract Making in Social Work Practice', in Stevenson, O. (ed.) *Trends in Social Work Education*, ATSWE/Alden Press.

Rooney, B. (1982) 'Black Social Workers in White Departments', in Juliet Cheetham (ed.) *Social Work and Ethnicity*, London, Allen & Unwin.

Sales, E. and Navarre, E. (1970) *Individual and Group Supervision in Field Instruction*.

Schlenoff, M. L. and Busa, S. H. (1981) 'Student and Field Instructor as Therapists: Equalizing an Unequal Relationship', *Journal of Education for Social Work*, vol. 17, no. 1.

Seebohm Report (1968) *Report of the Committee on Local Authority and Allied Personal Social Services*, London, HMSO.

Star, B. (1977) 'The Effects of Videotape Self-Image Confrontation on Helping Perceptions', *Journal of Education for Social Work*, vol. 13, no. 2, pp. 114–19.

Thomas, M. and Tierney, T. 'Student Contracts', *FSU Quarterly*, September 1982.

Toren, N. (1972) *Social Work as a Semi-Profession*, Beverly Hills, Sage.

Towle, C. (1954) *Learner in Education for the Professions*, University of Chicago Press.

Tyler, R. W. (1971) *Basic Principles of Curriculum and Instruction*, University of Chicago Press.

Westheimer, I. J. (1977) *The Practice of Supervision in Social Work. A Guide for Staff Supervisors*, London, Ward Lock Educational.

Whitehead, A. N. (1950) *The Aims of Education*, Williams & Norgate.

Wijnberg, M. H. and Schwartz, M. C. (1977) 'Models of Supervision: the Apprentice Growth and Role System Models', *Journal of Education for Social Work*, vol. 13, no. 3.

Yallom, J. (1969) *The Theory and Practice of Group Psychotherapy*, New York, Basic Books.

Young, P. (1967) *The Student And Supervision in Social Work Education*, London, Routledge & Kegan Paul.

Younghusband, E. (1978) *Social Work in Britain 1950–1975*, London, Allen & Unwin.

Index

159

162   *Index*